Bootstrap By Example

Master Bootstrap 4's frontend framework and build your websites faster than ever before

Silvio Moreto

BIRMINGHAM - MUMBAI

Bootstrap By Example

First published: March 2016

Production reference: 1230316

Published by Packt Publishing Ltd.
Livery Place
35 Livery Street
Birmingham B3 2PB, UK.

ISBN 978-1-78528-887-6

www.packtpub.com

Credits

Author
Silvio Moreto

Reviewer
Paula Barcante

Commissioning Editor
Ashwin Nair

Acquisition Editor
Smeet Thakkar

Content Development Editor
Pooja Mhapsekar

Technical Editor
Tanmayee Patil

Copy Editor
Vikrant Phadke

Project Coordinator
Francina Pinto

Proofreader
Safis Editing

Indexer
Monica Ajmera Mehta

Production Coordinator
Conidon Miranda

Cover Work
Conidon Miranda

About the Author

Silvio Moreto is a developer with more than 7 years of experience with frontend technologies and has created many websites and web applications using the Bootstrap framework. From simple pages to complex ones, he has always used the Bootstrap framework.

Silvio is also the creator of the bootstrap-select plugin (`http://silviomoreto.github.io/bootstrap-select/`), which is a very popular plugin among the community. It is for replacing a selected element by a Bootstrap button drop-down element. Silvio foresaw that a plugin like this one was missing in the original framework, and it could be useful for the community. So he created the plugin, and the community helps him maintain it.

Besides this, he is very active in the open source community, participating in some open source repository and issue communities, such as Stack Overflow. Also, he finished third in the worldwide Django Dash 2013 challenge.

First, I would like to thank my wife to supporting me throughout the writing process of the book. I would also like to thank my dog for staying beside me every night when I was writing and being the inspiration to some scenarios in the book. Then I want to thank the editors from Packt Publishing for their understanding and for guiding me through the completion of the book.

About the Reviewer

Paula Barcante is a 23 year old UX designer with a passion for frontend development. She learned development on her own by reading books and taking free online courses. She began using Bootstrap 4 years ago and has continued using it ever since. Paula's passion lies in designing and developing beautiful experiences for users around the world. Most recently, she began working as a UX designer for Amazon.com. She is always happy to chat with those who are passionate about design or frontend development. Her work can be found at `paulabarcante.com`.

www.PacktPub.com

eBooks, discount offers, and more

Did you know that Packt offers eBook versions of every book published, with PDF and ePub files available? You can upgrade to the eBook version at www.PacktPub.com and as a print book customer, you are entitled to a discount on the eBook copy. Get in touch with us at customercare@packtpub.com for more details.

At www.PacktPub.com, you can also read a collection of free technical articles, sign up for a range of free newsletters and receive exclusive discounts and offers on Packt books and eBooks.

https://www2.packtpub.com/books/subscription/packtlib

Do you need instant solutions to your IT questions? PacktLib is Packt's online digital book library. Here, you can search, access, and read Packt's entire library of books.

Why subscribe?

- Fully searchable across every book published by Packt
- Copy and paste, print, and bookmark content
- On demand and accessible via a web browser

Table of Contents

Preface

Frontend development can be separated into two eras, before Bootstrap and after Bootstrap. In 2011, the greatest frontend framework ever was released. Also, in the same year, the adoption and use of the framework grew in great numbers, reaching almost every segment of the market.

The reason of this is as follows: imagine how painful it was to create a simple, nice button, for instance. You had to declare a lot of classes and styles in your code. This was the foresee of Bootstrap, created by some developers from Twitter. The framework was a paradigm change for developing a fast-paced web page frontend.

The greatness of Bootstrap lies in three aspects. The first is the style sheet, which contains some basic CSS for almost every HTML element in a uniform and beauty way.

The second aspect is the components. They can be reused by just copying and pasting code. The last aspect is the JavaScript plugin, which includes some very common additional elements that cannot be found elsewhere.

Take a deep dive into the Bootstrap frontend framework with the help of examples that will illustrate the usage of each element and component in a proper way. By seeing examples, you will get a better understanding of what is happening and where you want to reach.

During the book, along the examples, you will be able to nail the framework and develop some very common examples using Bootstrap. These are a landing page, a web application, and a dashboard, which is desired by 10 out 10 web developers. You will face these kind of page countless number of times during your life as a developer, and you will do that using Bootstrap at its finest, including component customizations, animations, event handling, and external library integration.

We will start from the basics of the framework, but we will not hesitate from going further to really nail the framework. If you complete the book's examples by yourself, we can guarantee that you will become a true Bootstrap master.

This book is the first one to offer support for version 4 of Bootstrap. However, we will offer support for version 3 as well. So, you will be ready for whatever comes your way.

What this book covers

Chapter 1, Getting Started, introduces the Bootstrap framework and teaches you how to set up the environment.

Chapter 2, Creating a Solid Scaffolding, starts the landing page example using the grid system.

Chapter 3, Yes, You Should Go Mobile First, talks about mobile-first development and how to do it.

Chapter 4, Applying the Bootstrap Style, uses the Bootstrap theme and some Bootstrap elements.

Chapter 5, Making It Fancy, is about adding more Bootstrap elements to the landing page example.

Chapter 6, Can You Build a Web App?, challenges us to create a web application using Bootstrap.

Chapter 7, Of Course, You Can Build a Web App!, creates the web application page using only Bootstrap elements and components.

Chapter 8, Working with JavaScript, starts using some JavaScript plugins in the web application example.

Chapter 9, Entering in the Advanced Mode, is the start of the dashboard example using advanced components and plugin integrations.

Chapter 10, Bringing Components to Life, completes the dashboard example while making the final customizations for our web page.

Chapter 11, Making It Your Taste, is the final challenge, where we customize Bootstrap plugins and create a new plugin for the framework.

What you need for this book

To follow this book's developments, you will need a web browser on your computer, preferably Google Chrome, because it will be used in some examples. But other browsers can work as well.

Also, you will need some basic knowledge in HTML, CSS, and JavaScript beforehand. Despite the fact that we will initially talk in a slow pace about those technologies, it will be good for you to know some basic concepts about them.

Another plus is knowledge of the jQuery library, which is a dependency of Bootstrap. We will actually use jQuery in *Chapter 7, Of Course, You Can Build a Web App!*, and they will be very simple examples. So just keep in mind to train some jQuery skills.

Who this book is for

Bootstrap By Example is perfect for frontend developers interested in fast, mobile-first, and responsive development. Bootstrap is the most famous frontend framework, with a big community that needs you as a new member in this world of extensive support for different devices, resolutions, browsers, and ready-to-use components. With this book, you will acquire your ticket to it and play around like a pro.

Conventions

In this book, you will find a number of text styles that distinguish between different kinds of information. Here are some examples of these styles and an explanation of their meaning.

Code words in text, database table names, folder names, filenames, file extensions, pathnames, dummy URLs, user input, and Twitter handles are shown as follows: "Then, we created a `<div>` tag using the `.navbar-right` class to provide a set padding CSS rules and place the list to the right to appear the same way as before."

A block of code is set as follows:

```
<html>
  <head></head>
  <body>Hello World!</body>
</html>
```

When we wish to draw your attention to a particular part of a code block, the relevant lines or items are set in bold:

```
<html>
  <head></head>
  <body>Hello World!</body>
</html>
```

New terms and **important words** are shown in bold. Words that you see on the screen, for example, in menus or dialog boxes, appear in the text like this: "The preceding screenshot shows the final result of the **Features** section."

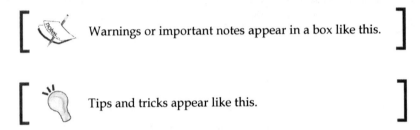

> Warnings or important notes appear in a box like this.

> Tips and tricks appear like this.

Reader feedback

Feedback from our readers is always welcome. Let us know what you think about this book—what you liked or disliked. Reader feedback is important for us as it helps us develop titles that you will really get the most out of.

To send us general feedback, simply e-mail feedback@packtpub.com, and mention the book's title in the subject of your message.

If there is a topic that you have expertise in and you are interested in either writing or contributing to a book, see our author guide at www.packtpub.com/authors.

Customer support

Now that you are the proud owner of a Packt book, we have a number of things to help you to get the most from your purchase.

Downloading the example code

You can download the example code files for this book from your account at
`http://www.packtpub.com`. If you purchased this book elsewhere, you can visit
`http://www.packtpub.com/support` and register to have the files e-mailed directly
to you.

You can download the code files by following these steps:

1. Log in or register to our website using your e-mail address and password.
2. Hover the mouse pointer on the **SUPPORT** tab at the top.
3. Click on **Code Downloads & Errata**.
4. Enter the name of the book in the **Search** box.
5. Select the book for which you're looking to download the code files.
6. Choose from the drop-down menu where you purchased this book from.
7. Click on **Code Download**.

Once the file is downloaded, please make sure that you unzip or extract the folder
using the latest version of:

- WinRAR / 7-Zip for Windows
- Zipeg / iZip / UnRarX for Mac
- 7-Zip / PeaZip for Linux

Downloading the color images of this book

We also provide you with a PDF file that has color images of the screenshots/
diagrams used in this book. The color images will help you better understand the
changes in the output. You can download this file from `https://www.packtpub.
com/sites/default/files/downloads/BootstrapByExample_ColorImages.pdf`.

Errata

Although we have taken every care to ensure the accuracy of our content, mistakes do happen. If you find a mistake in one of our books—maybe a mistake in the text or the code—we would be grateful if you could report this to us. By doing so, you can save other readers from frustration and help us improve subsequent versions of this book. If you find any errata, please report them by visiting http://www.packtpub.com/submit-errata, selecting your book, clicking on the **Errata Submission Form** link, and entering the details of your errata. Once your errata are verified, your submission will be accepted and the errata will be uploaded to our website or added to any list of existing errata under the Errata section of that title.

To view the previously submitted errata, go to https://www.packtpub.com/books/content/support and enter the name of the book in the search field. The required information will appear under the **Errata** section.

Piracy

Piracy of copyrighted material on the Internet is an ongoing problem across all media. At Packt, we take the protection of our copyright and licenses very seriously. If you come across any illegal copies of our works in any form on the Internet, please provide us with the location address or website name immediately so that we can pursue a remedy.

Please contact us at copyright@packtpub.com with a link to the suspected pirated material.

We appreciate your help in protecting our authors and our ability to bring you valuable content.

Questions

If you have a problem with any aspect of this book, you can contact us at questions@packtpub.com, and we will do our best to address the problem.

1
Getting Started

With the advent and increase in popularity of the mobile web, developers have had to adapt themselves to handling new challenges, such as different layouts in different resolutions, the new user experience paradigm, and optimization for low-bandwidth connections. While facing this, there were also a lot of old problems related to browser compatibility and lack of patterns in the community.

This was the outline scenario when the Bootstrap framework arrived. Developed by Twitter, the main goal of Bootstrap is to provide a web frontend framework for responsive developing with cross-browser compatibility. It is awesome! Developers fell in love with it and started to adopt it right away.

Therefore, to cover this book's objective of presenting the Bootstrap framework to build responsive, mobile-first websites faster than ever before, we must get started by setting up our work environment in the best recommended way. Thus, the topics that we will cover in this chapter are:

- Getting Bootstrap
- Setting up Bootstrap in a web page
- Building the first Bootstrap example
- The container element tag
- Support sources
- Framework compatibility

Getting Bootstrap

There is some version of the framework, but in this book, we will provide support for the latest Bootstrap 3 version (which is v3.3.5), along with the newest version 4 (which is 4.0.0-alpha). When a feature or component is differently supported by one of these versions, we will point it out properly.

First of all, access the official website at `http://getbootstrap.com/` and click on the **Download Bootstrap** button, as shown in the following screenshot:

Downloading the example code

You can download the example code files for this book from your account at `http://www.packtpub.com`. If you purchased this book elsewhere, you can visit `http://www.packtpub.com/support` and register to have the files e-mailed directly to you.

You can download the code files by following these steps:

- Log in or register to our website using your e-mail address and password.
- Hover the mouse pointer on the **SUPPORT** tab at the top.
- Click on **Code Downloads & Errata**.
- Enter the name of the book in the **Search** box.
- Select the book for which you're looking to download the code files.
- Choose from the drop-down menu where you purchased this book from.
- Click on **Code Download**.

Once the file is downloaded, please make sure that you unzip or extract the folder using the latest version of:

- WinRAR / 7-Zip for Windows
- Zipeg / iZip / UnRarX for Mac
- 7-Zip / PeaZip for Linux

Then you will be redirected to another page that contains these buttons:

- **Download Bootstrap**: This is the release with the files already compiled.
- **Download source**: Use this if you want to get the source for customization. This requires knowledge of the Less language.
- **Download Sass**: Here, you can get the source code in the Sass language.

Click on the **Download Bootstrap** button to get the framework, since we will cover the full framework using, not Sass, but just HTML, CSS, and JavaScript. After the download, extract the files and you will see that the framework is organized in folders.

Other versions and releases

Check out the official repository at `https://github.com/twbs/bootstrap/` to pick up other versions and see the new releases under development. You will also be able to see other features and community activity.

If you want to go hands-on straightforward with version 4, go to `http://v4-alpha.getbootstrap.com/` and download it, or enter the GitHub repository and select the corresponding branch of version 4.

After you've extracted the files, you will see some folders. The first one, in alphabetical order, is `css`. Here, you will find the main CSS file (named `bootstrap.css`), other files related to the minified version, and a `bootstrap-theme.css` file, which is a simple theme of using the Bootstrap components.

There is also a `fonts` folder; it contains the files used for the icon components that we will see in future chapters. Finally, there is a folder named `js`, where we can find the `bootstrap.js` file, the minified version, and the specification for `npm`.

What is the npm file?

The npm is the most famous package manager for JavaScript. It is set as the default package manager in the Node.js environment.

Setting up the framework

Now that we have downloaded the framework and covered its basic file architecture, we will advance to setting up Bootstrap on a web page.

Folder structure

First, let's explicit the folder structure that we will be using in this book. In a folder that we will call `main_folder`, we extract the Bootstrap contents and create a file called `hello_world.html` at the same level. Inside the Bootstrap contents will be some folders for fonts, CSS, and JavaScript. The final layout should be like this:

```
main_folder
-   hello_world.html
-   css
        -   bootstrap.css
-   fonts
        -   glyphicons-halflings-regular.eot
        -   glyphicons-halflings-regular.svg
        -   glyphicons-halflings-regular.ttf
        -   glyphicons-halflings-regular.woff

        -   glyphicons-halflings-regular.woff2
-   js
        -   bootstrap.js
```

Warming up the sample example

Now, we will add the recommended setup of the Bootstrap framework to the `hello_world.html` file. Open it in your preferred code editor and add the outline HTML code, like this:

```html
<!DOCTYPE html>
<html>
<head>
    <title>Hello World!</title>
</head>
<body>
    Hello World
</body>
</html>
```

Next, add the code for loading `css` inside the `head` tag:

```html
<!DOCTYPE html>
<html>
<head>
    <title>Hello World!</title>
    <link rel="stylesheet" href="css/bootstrap.css">
```

```
</head>
<body>
    Hello World
</body>
</html>
```

And at the end of the body tag, load the JavaScript file:

```
<!DOCTYPE html>
<html>
<head>
    <title>Hello World!</title>
    <link rel="stylesheet" href="css/bootstrap.css">
</head>
<body>
    Hello World
    <script src="js/bootstrap.js"></script>
</body>
</html>
```

Open the hello_world.html file in a browser (we will use Google Chrome in this book) and open the JavaScript console. In Chrome, it can be found at *Options* button (the hamburger button on right upper corner. Go to **More Tools | Developer Tools**, just as shown in the following screenshot, and click on **Console** in the opened window. You will see a message saying **Bootstrap's JavaScript requires jQuery**:

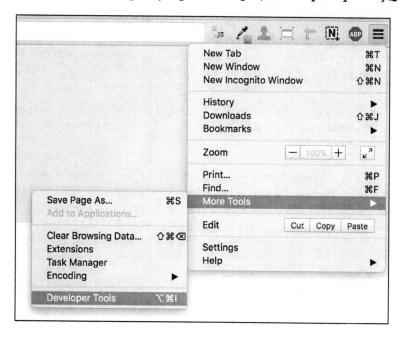

jQuery is a cross-platform JavaScript library, and it is the only third-party requirement for Bootstrap. To get it, we recommend the download from the official website and the latest version (`https://jquery.com/download/`). Bootstrap requires version 1.9 or higher.

 Just use versions above 2.x if you do not want to add support for Internet Explorer 6, 7, and 8. In this book, we will use version 1.11.3.

Copy the jQuery file inside the `js` folder, and load it in the HTML code at the end of the body tag but before the `bootstrap.js` loads, like this:

```
<script src="js/jquery-1.11.3.js"></script>
<script src="js/bootstrap.js"></script>
```

Bootstrap required tags

Bootstrap has three tags that must be at the beginning of the `<head>` tag. These tags are used for text encoding and improved visualization on mobile devices:

```
<meta charset="utf-8">
<meta http-equiv="X-UA-Compatible" content="IE=edge">
<meta name="viewport" content="width=device-width, initial-scale=1">
```

The `viewport` tag is related to the mobile-first philosophy. By adding it, you ensure proper rendering in mobile devices and touch zooming.

You can also disable the zoom functionality by appending `user-scalable=no` in the content key. With this option, users will only be able to scroll on the web page, resulting in a feel of using a native mobile application.

 If you are going to use this tag, you must be sure that users need not use the zoom feature and it will create a good user experience. Therefore, use it with caution.

Also, if you want to add support for older versions of the Internet Explorer (IE) browser (older than version 9), you must add some libraries to have fallback compatibility for the HTML5 and CSS3 elements. We will add them via CDN, which is the Bootstrap recommendation. So, add these lines at the end of the `<head>` tag:

```
<!--[if lt IE 9]>
    <script
src="https://oss.maxcdn.com/html5shiv/3.7.2/html5shiv.min.js"></
script>
```

```
    <script
src="https://oss.maxcdn.com/respond/1.4.2/respond.min.js">
</script> <![endif]-->
```

Do you know what CDN is?

CDN, the abbreviation of **Content Delivery Network**, is a term used to describe a network of computers that are connected in order to deliver some content. A CDN should provide high availability and performance.

At this point, the file should be like this:

```
<!DOCTYPE html>
<html>
  <head>
    <meta charset="utf-8">
    <meta http-equiv="X-UA-Compatible" content="IE=edge">
    <meta name="viewport" content="width=device-width,
initial-scale=1">
    <title>Hello World!</title>

    <link rel="stylesheet" href="css/bootstrap.css">

    <!--[if lt IE 9]>
      <script
src="https://oss.maxcdn.com/html5shiv/3.7.2/html5shiv.min.js">
      </script>
      <script
src="https://oss.maxcdn.com/respond/1.4.2/respond.min.js">
      </script>
    <![endif]-->
  </head>
  <body>
    Hello World!

    <script src="js/jquery-1.11.3.js"></script>
    <script src="js/bootstrap.js"></script>
  </body>
</html>
```

This is our base page example! Keep it for the purpose of coding every example of this book and for any other web page that you will develop.

We would like to point out that Bootstrap requires the doctype HTML5 style before the <html> tag:

```
<!DOCTYPE html>
<html>
    ... <!--rest of the HTML code -->
</html>
```

Building our first Bootstrap example

Now we are all set for the framework. Replace the Hello World! line in the body tag with this:

```
<!DOCTYPE html>
<html>
  <head>
    <meta charset="utf-8">
    <meta http-equiv="X-UA-Compatible" content="IE=edge">
    <meta name="viewport" content="width=device-width, initial-
scale=1">
    <title>Hello World!</title>

    <link rel="stylesheet" href="css/bootstrap.css">

    <!--[if lt IE 9]>
       <script
src="https://oss.maxcdn.com/html5shiv/3.7.2/html5shiv.min.js">
</script>
       <script
src="https://oss.maxcdn.com/respond/1.4.2/respond.min.js">
</script>
    <![endif]-->
  </head>
  <body>

    <div class="jumbotron">
      <h1>Hello, world!</h1>
      <p>This is our first sample example that will be more
awesome in the next chapters!</p>
        <a class="btn btn-primary btn-lg" href="#" role="button">
          Bootstrap by Example, Chapter 1
```

```
      </a>
    </div>


    <script src="js/jquery-1.11.3.js"></script>
    <script src="js/bootstrap.js"></script>
  </body>
</html>
```

Open the `hello_world.html` file in the browser, and it must appear like what is shown in the following screenshot:

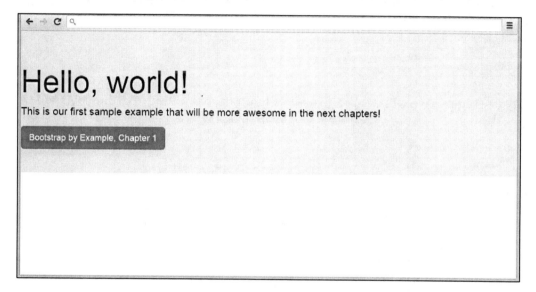

Congratulations! You have created your first Bootstrap web page. It is simple but very important to understand the details of how to set the framework correctly to keep the recommendation pattern.

Furthermore, we added some components in this example that will be explained in future chapters, but you can start becoming familiar with the CSS classes used and the placement of the elements.

The container tag

You may notice that in our example, the page content is too close to the left-hand side and without a margin/padding. This is because Bootstrap has a required element called `container` that we have not added in the example.

The `container` tag must be placed to wrap the site content and nest the grid system (we will present the grid system, called scaffolding, in the next chapter). There are two options for using the container element.

The first one is for creating a web page responsive with a fixed-width container. This one will add responsive margins depending on the device viewport:

```html
<div class="container">
   ...
</div>
```

In case you want a full-width container, covering the entire width of the viewport, use `container-fluid`:

```html
<div class="container-fluid">
   ...
</div>
```

In our example, we will create a fixed-width responsive website. So, our code will be like this:

```html
<!DOCTYPE html>
<html>
  <head>
    <meta charset="utf-8">
    <meta http-equiv="X-UA-Compatible" content="IE=edge">
    <meta name="viewport" content="width=device-width, initial-scale=1">
    <title>Hello World!</title>

    <link rel="stylesheet" href="css/bootstrap.css">

    <!--[if lt IE 9]>
      <script src="https://oss.maxcdn.com/html5shiv/3.7.2/html5shiv.min.js">
</script>
      <script
src="https://oss.maxcdn.com/respond/1.4.2/respond.min.js">
</script>
    <![endif]-->
  </head>
  <body>
    <div class="container">
        <div class="jumbotron">
            <h1>Hello, world!</h1>
```

```
        <p>This is our first sample example that will be more
awesome in the next chapters!</p>
        <a class="btn btn-primary btn-lg" href="#"
role="button">
            Bootstrap by Example, Chapter 1
        </a>
      </div>
    </div>

    <script src="js/jquery-1.11.3.js"></script>
    <script src="js/bootstrap.js"></script>
  </body>
</html>
```

The next screenshot shows what our example looks like with the addition of the container class. I recommend for practicing and complete understanding, that you change the container class to .container-fluid and see what happens. Change your viewport by resizing your browser window and see how Bootstrap adapts your page visualization:

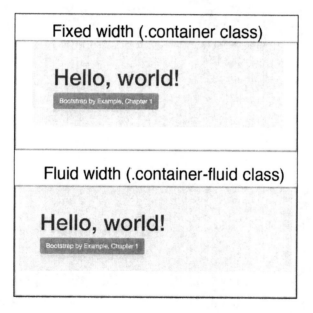

The preceding image shows the differences between using .container and .container-fluid. See the differences of the margins in the sides.

Soon during this book, you will be able to create more complex and beautiful websites, using more advanced Bootstrap components such as the show case shown in the following screenshot, which is an example of a landing page.

Do not worry. We will start at a slow pace to reveal the basics of Bootstrap and how to use it properly on our web page. The following example is our first goal when we develop a landing page example. Just keep in mind that we will always use the same basis presented in this chapter.

Optionally using the CDN setup

Bootstrap also offers a setup using CDN to load the framework. It's much easier to set up but comes with some regards. Instead of the <link> that we created to load the CSS, we must load it from CDN using this:

```
<link rel="stylesheet"
href="https://maxcdn.bootstrapcdn.com/bootstrap/3.3.5/css/
bootstrap.min.css">
```

And to load the JavaScript file, replace the JavaScript `<script>` tag with the following line:

```
<script
src="https://maxcdn.bootstrapcdn.com/bootstrap/3.3.5/js/bootstrap.min.
js"></script>
```

There is some discussion on whether or not to use CDN. We will not touch upon this point, but the main pro is having the content provided faster with high availability. The main con is that you cannot have direct control over what is in the content provided, having unreliable imported code.

The decision of whether or not to use CDN depends on the case. You should consider the different arguments and choose an option that best fits your web page. There is no right or wrong, just different points of view.

Community activity

The Bootstrap framework is discussed in several places across the Internet. It is important to have an engaged community that keeps evolving the framework and supporting it. You can have support and acquire more knowledge by going to some other resources, such as the following:

- The Bootstrap official GitHub repository. Here (`https://github.com/twbs/bootstrap`), you can find the road map development and the newest releases, report issues, and solve them by making a pull request.

- The Bootstrap official documentation (`http://getbootstrap.com/`) provides some additional information of the framework's usage and support.

- Bootstrap Blog (`http://blog.getbootstrap.com/`) is the best way to follow news about Bootstrap and read the releases notes.

- Bootstrap Expo (`http://expo.getbootstrap.com/`) is a showcase web page where you can see some beautiful websites that use the framework and resources to be used within such as plugins, themes, and so on.

- Stack Overflow questions related to Bootstrap (`http://stackoverflow.com/questions/tagged/twitter-bootstrap`). This is one of the best means of communication to get help from for your issues. Search for questions related to yours, and if you can't find something related, I guarantee that you will have an answer very soon.

There are many other resources spread across the Internet. Use them all to your advantage, and appreciate the taste of developing in fast pace with the best frontend framework of our time.

Tools

Bootstrap has an official HTML lint called Bootlint (`https://github.com/twbs/bootlint`). It checks the DOM for mistakes in using Bootstrap elements and components. Add Bootlint to avoid mistakes that delay your development. Check out the repository for installation and usage instructions.

Bootstrap and web applications

Bootstrap is one of the best frameworks for building web apps. Since you may use the same layout pattern across the web app, with premade classes and themes provided by the framework, you can speed up your development while maintaining the coherence of the elements used.

After the framework's release, Twitter adopted it like many other web apps as well. The following screenshot shows a great example of a fluid web app that uses Bootstrap with a fluid container:

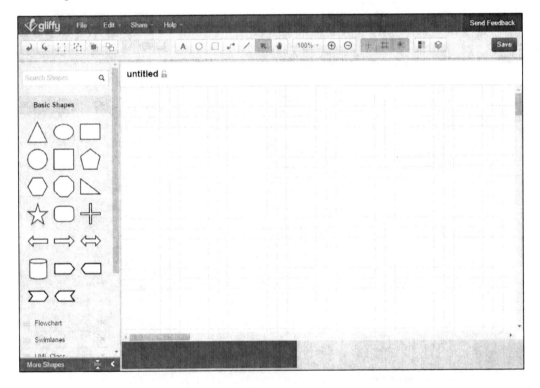

Browser compatibility

The Bootstrap framework supports the most recent versions of the most used browsers. However, depending on the browser, the elements' rendering might look a little different from others, such as in the Chrome and Firefox Linux versions.

Internet Explorer's (IE) old versions do not have some properties from CSS3 and HTML5 that are used in the framework, so be aware of this when supporting these browsers. The following table presents the official browser compatibility.

Also, with the new version 4 of the framework, some compatibilities have been dropped. They decided to drop the support that existed for IE8, since it was dragging down the addition of new features, and now Bootstrap is able to take advantage of the use of some new CSS features.

With regard to this, version 4 moved from pixels to rems and ems measures to make responsive and resizing easier, and with that, they dropped support for iOS 6 as well:

	Chrome	Firefox	Internet Explorer	Opera	Safari
Android	Yes	Yes	N/A	No	N/A
iOS	Yes	N/A	N/A	No	Yes (iOS 7 + for v4)
OS X	Yes	Yes	N/A	Yes	Yes
Windows	Yes	Yes	Yes (IE9 + for v4)	Yes	No

The meaning of em and rem

The units em and rem have moved from trending to reality! They are enforced as present in our context and have now gained the support of Bootstrap. The main difference between em and rem is that they are relative unit metrics, while pixels are not. em is a unit relative to the parent font size and rem is a unit relative to the root element, perfectly fitting this responsivity development context.

Summary

In this chapter, you learned some basic concepts about using the Bootstrap framework. These are the key points for creating web sites with high quality. Knowing them in depth gives you a huge advantage and helps with the handling of future problems.

The chapter's goal was to show the recommended setup for the Bootstrap framework, presenting the placement of the tags, libraries import, and creating a very simple web page. Remember that consistency across the website is the main thing about Bootstrap, saving your precious time.

Also keep in mind that when starting a new web page, you have to guarantee a good placement of the main tags and components no matter how you created it (manually, boilerplate, or in other ways). Many problems stem from inadequate groundwork.

We also presented some resources from which you can acquire further knowledge or any kind of help. You now belong to a big "open arms" community that you can always count on.

Now that we have this background, let's attack some real-world problems! In the next chapter, we will start developing a very common real-life example, which is a landing page, while presenting some Bootstrap components, HTML elements, and grid systems.

2
Creating a Solid Scaffolding

In this chapter, you will start learning some new Bootstrap elements and components. By doing this, you will first understand the concepts of the Bootstrap grid system and move on to some basic components. Now, we are going to start the development of a responsive sample landing page. First, we will use the base theme of the framework, and in future, we will apply our own style.

The main structure of this chapter is as follows:

- The Bootstrap grid system
- Typography
- Tables
- Buttons

Understanding the grid system

The basis of the Bootstrap framework relies in its grid system. Bootstrap offers components that allow us to structure a website in a responsive grid layout.

To exemplify this, imagine an electronic square sheet table that can be divided into many rows and columns, as shown in the following screenshot. In the table, you can create as many lines as you want while merging cells. But what would happen if you wanted to change the layout of a single row? That could be painful.

	A	B	C	D	E
1			Sauce year selling		
2			2014	2015	Total
3		Restaurants	12000	18000	30000
4	Ketchup	Black market	5000	7500	12500
5		Reatilers	48500	72750	121250
6	Mustard	Black market	6590	9885	16475
7		Retailers	1576	2364	3940
8	Relish	Black market	589600	884400	1474000
9			663266	994899	1658165
10					

The Bootstrap grid system works in a different way. By letting you define a set of rows, each one having a set of independent columns, it allows you to build a solid grid system for your web page. Also, each column can have different sizes to perfectly fit your template.

This not being enough, the Bootstrap grid system adapts for every viewport and resolution, which we call responsiveness.

To start learning about the grid system, we will introduce it using the example of a landing page. As you will see, Bootstrap will allow us to create a complete scaffolding that will automatically adjust the content for any viewport.

Building our scaffolding

For our landing page, we will use the grid presented in the following image. As you can see, it is represented by seven rows, each containing a different number of columns. In this first example, we will use a nonmobile viewport, which we will discuss in the next chapter.

1	**HEADER**		
2	1/3 offset	1/3	1/3
3	1/3	2/3	
4	1/4	1/2	1/4
5	1/4	1/4	1/4	1/4
6	1/4	1/4	1/4	1/4
7	1/6	7/12	1/4

Setting things up

To start that, let's use our default layout presented in *Chapter 1, Getting Started*. Add inside the `div.container` tag another `div` with the `.row` class:

```
<!DOCTYPE html>
<html>
  <head>
    <meta charset="utf-8">
    <meta http-equiv="X-UA-Compatible" content="IE=edge">
    <meta name="viewport" content="width=device-width, initial-
scale=1">
    <title>Landing page</title>

    <link rel="stylesheet" href="css/bootstrap.css">

    <!--[if lt IE 9]>
      <script
src="https://oss.maxcdn.com/html5shiv/3.7.2/html5shiv.min.js">
</script>
```

```
    <script
src="https://oss.maxcdn.com/respond/1.4.2/respond.min.js">
</script>
    <![endif]-->
  </head>
  <body>
    <div class="container">
      <div class="row"></div>
    </div>

    <script src="js/jquery-1.11.3.js"></script>
    <script src="js/bootstrap.js"></script>
  </body>
</html>
```

The hierarchy for the grid system always follows the sequence of a container that wraps rows and multiple columns. Keep in mind to always use this sequence to get a proper output.

Now that we have our .container with the first .row, let's create our first column. Every row is subdivided into 12 parts, so you can have up to 12 columns in a single row.

To identify a column, we must follow the template of .col-*-*. The first asterisk means the viewport for the column, and the other one means the size of the column. We will explain more about that, but to create our first column, we create a column identified by .col-md-12 inside our row:

```
<div class="container">
  <div class="row">
    <header class="col-md-12">
      HEADER
    </header>
  </div>
</div>
```

In this column, the md in .col-md-12 means that for the viewport medium (which means the md identifier), the column must have a 12-column width. In other words, the column fills the entire width of this row. This column will fill the complete width because it is our header, and as we can see in the previous image, this row is composed of just a single row.

So, to create a column in the Bootstrap grid system, you must follow the recipe of `.col-*-*` for every column. While you can set an integer from 1 to 12 for the width, for the viewport, you must set the correct class prefix. In this table, you can see the breakdown of class prefix usage and on which resolution it can be used:

	Extra small devices (phones < 544 px / 34 em)	Small devices (tablets ≥ 544 px / 34 em and < 768 px / 48 em)	Medium devices (desktops ≥ 768 px /48 em and < 900 px / 62 em)	Large devices (desktops ≥ 900 px / 62 em and < 1,200 px 75 em)	Extra large devices (desktops ≥ 1,200 px / 75 em)
Grid behavior	Horizontal lines at all times	Collapse at start and fit the column grid			
Container's fixed width	Auto	544 px or 34 rem	750 px or 45 rem	970 px or 60 rem	1170 px or 72.25 rem
Class prefix	`.col-xs-*`	`.col-sm-*`	`.col-md-*`	`.col-lg-*`	`.col-xl-*`
Number of columns	12				
Column fixed width	Auto	~ 44 px or 2.75 rem	~ 62 px or 3.86 rem	~ 81 px or 5.06 rem	~ 97 px or 6.06 rem

What will happen if I create a row with more than 12 columns?

Try adding a number of columns with a number higher than 12, for instance, five columns with the `.col-md-3` class. Knowing that every row is treated as a unit of 12 columns, the next ones will wrap in a new line.

Offset columns

Our second row is divided into three equal-sized columns, and the first one is an offset column, or in other words, an empty column that will be filled by a left margin. Therefore, the second row will be like this:

```
<div class="row">
    <div class="col-md-offset-4 col-md-4">1/3</div>
    <div class="col-md-4">1/3</div>
</div>
```

As you can see, by adding the `.col-md-offset-4` class, we create a margin to the left four, sized in just this `.row`. By having each row independent of the others, we can properly customize the layout to appear just as it is supposed to be.

What happens if I add more than two offsets in a single column?

If you do that, you will find yourself in a funny situation. As a tip, only one offset is applied for an element, but which one? The answer is, the smallest offset!

Completing the grid rows

Now we will advance to the third row in our scaffolding. If you've got the spirit, you should have no problems with this row. For training, try doing it by yourself and check the solution in the book afterwards! I am sure you can handle it.

So, this row is composed of two columns. The first column must fill 4 out of the 12 parts of the row and the other column will fill the rest. The row in the HTML should look like this:

```
<div class="row">
  <div class="col-md-4"></div>
  <div class="col-md-8"></div>
</div>
```

About the fourth row — it is composed of a quarter divisor, followed by a half divisor, followed by a last quarter divisor. Using this in base 12, we will have the following grid in the row:

```
<div class="row">
  <div class="col-md-3">1/4</div>
  <div class="col-md-6">1/2</div>
  <div class="col-md-3">1/4</div>
</div>
```

Nesting rows

In the fifth and sixth rows, we will show how you can create a row using two options. In the fifth row, we will create just as we are doing in the other rows, while in the sixth row, we will use the concept of nesting rows.

So, in the fifth row, create it just as you were doing before; create a row with four equally sized rows, which means that each column will have the `.col-md-3` class:

```
<div class="row">
  <div class="col-md-3">1/4</div>
  <div class="col-md-3">1/4</div>
  <div class="col-md-3">1/4</div>
  <div class="col-md-3">1/4</div>
</div>
```

For the sixth row, we will use nesting rows. So, let's create the first `.row`, having three columns:

```
<div class="row">
  <div class="col-md-3">1/4</div>
  <div class="col-md-6"></div>
  <div class="col-md-3">1/4</div>
</div>
```

As you can see, the first and the last column use the same class of columns in row five — the `.col-md-3` class — while the middle column is double the size, with the `.col-md-6` class.

Let's nest another `.row` inside the middle column. When you create a new nested row, the columns inside of it are refreshed and you have another set of 12-sized columns to put inside it. So, inside this new row, create two columns with the `.col-md-6` class to generate two columns representing a fourth of the row:

```
<div class="row">
  <div class="col-md-3">1/4</div>
  <div class="col-md-6">
    <div class="row">
      <div class="col-md-6">1/4</div>
      <div class="col-md-6">1/4</div>
    </div>
  </div>
  <div class="col-md-3">1/4</div>
</div>
```

The concept of nesting rows is pretty complex, since you can infinitely subdivide a row, although it is great to create small grid components inside your page that can be used in other locations.

Finishing the grid

To create the last row, we need to create the `.col-md-2` column, followed by `.col-md-7` and `.col-md-3`. So, just create a row using the `<footer>` tag with those columns. The complete scaffolding will be this:

```html
<!DOCTYPE html>
<html>
  <head>
    <meta charset="utf-8">
    <meta http-equiv="X-UA-Compatible" content="IE=edge">
    <meta name="viewport" content="width=device-width, initial-scale=1">
    <title>Landing page</title>
    <link rel="stylesheet" href="css/bootstrap.css">
    <!--[if lt IE 9]>
      <script src="https://oss.maxcdn.com/html5shiv/3.7.2/html5shiv.min.js"></script>
      <script src="https://oss.maxcdn.com/respond/1.4.2/respond.min.js"></script>
    <![endif]-->
  </head>
  <body>
    <div class="container">
      <!-- row 1 -->
      <div class="row">
        <header class="col-md-12">
          HEADER
        </header>
      </div>

      <!-- row 2 -->
      <div class="row">
        <div class="col-md-offset-4 col-md-4">1/3</div>
        <div class="col-md-4">1/3</div>
      </div>

      <!-- row 3 -->
      <div class="row">
        <div class="col-md-4"></div>
        <div class="col-md-8"></div>
      </div>
```

```
    <!-- row 4 -->
    <div class="row">
      <div class="col-md-3">1/4</div>
      <div class="col-md-6">1/2</div>
      <div class="col-md-3">1/4</div>
    </div>

    <!-- row 5 -->
    <div class="row">
      <div class="col-md-3">1/4</div>
      <div class="col-md-3">1/4</div>
      <div class="col-md-3">1/4</div>
      <div class="col-md-3">1/4</div>
    </div>

    <!-- row 6 - nesting rows -->
    <div class="row">
      <div class="col-md-3">1/4</div>
      <div class="col-md-6">
        <div class="row">
          <div class="col-md-6">1/4</div>
          <div class="col-md-6">1/4</div>
        </div>
      </div>
      <div class="col-md-3">1/4</div>
    </div>

    <!-- row 7 -->
    <footer class="row">
      <div class="col-md-2">1/2</div>
      <div class="col-md-7">7/12</div>
      <div class="col-md-3">1/4</div>
    </footer>
  </div>

  <script src="js/jquery-1.11.3.js"></script>
  <script src="js/bootstrap.js"></script>
  </body>
</html>
```

Fluid container

You can easily switch the actual example grid with a fluid full-width layout. To do so, replace the farthest `.container` with `.container-fluid`:

```
<div class="container-fluid">
  ...
</div>
```

We need some style!

Now, we will start using some of the CSS provided for Bootstrap to make our components responsive and more elegant. Our main goal is to make our grid page like what is shown in this screenshot:

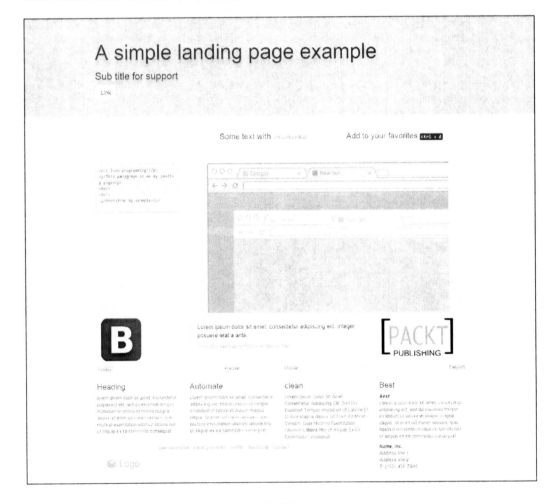

Let's break down each row and learn about typography and some other components. We will do this without using a single custom line of CSS!

Getting started with the first row, you may see that this row has a gray background, which is not present in the rest of the layout. To create this, we must make a change in our grid by creating a new `.container` for this row. So, create another `.container` and place it inside the first row:

```
<div class="container">
  <!-- row 1 -->
  <div class="row">
    <header class="col-md-12">
    </header>
  </div>
</div>
<div class="container">
  <!-- the others rows (2 to 7) -->
</div>
```

Now, to make the gray area, we will use a class in Bootstrap called `.jumbotron`. The `jumbotron` is a flexible Bootstrap component that can extend to the entire viewport to showcase some content, in this case the header. So, wrap the container inside a `div.jumbotron`:

```
<div class="jumbotron">
  <div class="container">
    <!-- row 1 -->
    <div class="row">
      <header class="col-md-12">
      </header>
    </div>
  </div>
</div>
```

Inside the header, as we can see in the layout, we must create a title, a subtitle, and a button. For the title, let's use the `<h1>` and `<h2>` heading elements. For the button, let's create a link with the `.btn`, `.btn-default`, and `.btn-lg` classes. We will mention more about these components in the next subsections:

```
<div class="jumbotron">
  <div class="container">
    <!-- row 1 -->
    <div class="row">
      <header class="col-md-12">
        <h1>A simple landing page example</h1>
```

```
            <h2>Sub title for support</h2>
            <a class="btn btn-default btn-lg" href="#" role="button">
              Link
            </a>
          </header>
        </div>
      </div>
    </div>
```

There are headings everywhere

Bootstrap provides styled headings from h1 to h6. You should always use them in order of importance, from `<h1>` to `<h6>` (the least important).

Do you know why headings are important?

Heading are very important for **Search Engine Optimization (SEO)**. They suggest for search engines what is important in your page context. You must keep the hierarchy for page coherence, and do not skip any tag (that is, jump from heading 3 to heading 5). Otherwise, the structure will be broken and not relevant for SEO.

The heading has classes for identifying its style. So, if your most important phrase is not the biggest one at times, you can swap the sizes by adding heading classes, just as in the following example:

```
<h1 class="h3">Heading 1 styled as heading 3</h1>
<h2 class="h1">Heading 2 styled as heading 1</h2>
<h3 class="h2">Heading 3 styled as heading 2</h3>
```

Heading 1 styled as heading 3

Heading 2 styled as heading 1

Heading 3 styled as heading 2

Playing with buttons

The other element of the first row is a button! We can apply button classes for hyperlinks, button elements, and inputs. To make one of these elements a button, just add the `.btn` class followed by the kind of button, in this case the kind `.btn-default`, which is a blue button. The next table shows every possibility of color classes for a button:

Button class	Output
`.btn-default`	Default
`.btn-primary`	Primary
`.btn-success`	Success
`.btn-info`	Info
`.btn-warning`	Warning
`.btn-danger`	Danger
`.btn-link`	Link

We have also added the `.btn-lg` class in the first row button. This class will increase the size of the button. Bootstrap also provides some other button size classes, such as `.btn-sm` for small buttons and `.btn-xs` for even smaller ones.

You can also make a button span the full width of the parent element with the `.btn-block` class, changing the display of the button to `block`.

More typography and code tags

With regards to the second row, we have a row that contains a heading and complementary small text after that.

To add lighter and secondary text to the heading, we can add a `<small>` tag or any other tag with the `.small` class inside the heading. The HTML for the first column in the second row should be like the following:

```
<div class="row">
  <div class="col-md-offset-4 col-md-4">
    <h3>
      Some text with <small>secondary text</small>
    </h3>
  </div>
  <div class="col-md-4">
    <h3>
      Add to your favorites
      <small>
        <kbd><kbd>ctrl</kbd> + <kbd>d</kbd></kbd>
      </small>
    </h3>
  </div>
</div>
```

Note that inside the small tag, we have added a `<kbd>` tag, which is an HTML element that creates a user-like input keyboard. Refresh the web browser and you will see this row as shown here:

Some text with secondary text   Add to your favorites `ctrl + d`

For the third row, we have a code snippet and an image. To create a code snippet, use the `<pre>` tag for multiple lines of code. The `<pre>` tag is present in HTML for creating preformatted text, such as a code snippet. You have the option of adding the `.pre-scrollable` class, which will add a scrollbar if the code snippet reaches the maximum height of 350 px (or 21.8 em).

For this row, in the right column, we have an image. For that, just create an `<img>` tag and add the `.img-responsive` class, which will make the images automatically responsive-friendly to the viewport. The HTML for the third row is as follows:

```
<div class="row">
  <div class="col-md-3">
    <pre>&lt;p&gt;I love programming!&lt;/p&gt;
&lt;p&gt;This paragraph is on my landing page&lt;/p&gt;
&lt;br/&gt;
&lt;br/&gt;
&lt;p&gt;Bootstrap by example&lt;/p&gt;
    </pre>
  </div>
  <div class="col-md-9">
    <img src="imgs/center.png" class="img-responsive">
  </div>
</div>
```

Refresh your browser and you will see the result of this row as shown in the following screenshot:

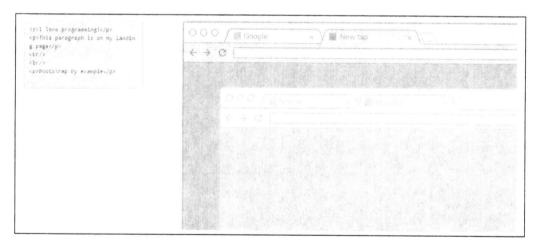

In the fourth row, we have images in both the left and right columns and a testimonial in the middle. Bootstrap provides a typographic theme for doing block quotes, so just create a `<blockquote>` tag. Inside it, create a `<footer>` tag to identify the source, and wrap the name in a `<cite>` tag, like this:

```
<div class="row">
  <div class="col-md-3">
    <img src="imgs/bs.png" class="img-responsive">
  </div>
  <div class="col-md-6">
    <blockquote>
      <p>Lorem ipsum dolor sit amet, consectetur adipiscing elit.
Integer posuere erat a ante.</p>
      <footer>Testimonial from someone at <cite title="Source
Title">Source Title</cite></footer>
    </blockquote>
  </div>
  <div class="col-md-3">
    <img src="imgs/packt.png" class="img-responsive">
  </div>
</div>
```

Lorem ipsum dolor sit amet, consectetur adipiscing elit. Integer posuere erat a ante.
— Testimonial from someone at *Source Title*

Moving on, we must advance to the fifth row. This row is here just to show the different ways in which we can apply typography and coding elements tags using Bootstrap. Let's go through each one to describe its usage.

In the first column, we have a piece of inline code. To do that, wrap the snippet in a `<code>` tag. From the first to the fourth column of this row, we are presenting the alignment classes. Using these, you can easily realign text content in a paragraph tag. The code for the row is as follows:

```
<div class="row">
  <div class="col-md-3">
    <p class="text-left"><code>&lt;Left&gt;</code></p>
  </div>
  <div class="col-md-3">
    <p class="text-center">Center</p>
  </div>
  <div class="col-md-3">
    <p class="text-justify">Jusitfy</p>
```

```
  </div>
  <div class="col-md-3">
    <p class="text-right">Right</p>
  </div>
</div>
```

Just use the right classes for a proper alignment. The result in the browser should look like this:

The sixth row is composed of four equally divided columns, but in this case, we are using the nesting rows option. On the first three columns, we added Bootstrap text transformation classes to make the text lowercase, uppercase, and capitalized, respectively. The code for this row should be like the following:

```
<div class="row">
  <div class="col-md-3">
    <h3>Lowercase</h3>
    <p class="text-lowercase">
      Lorem ipsum dolor ... consequat.
    </p>
  </div>
  <div class="col-md-6">
    <div class="row">
      <div class="col-md-6">
        <h3>Uppercase</h3>
        <p class="text-uppercase">
          Lorem ipsum dolor ... consequat.
        </p>
      </div>
      <div class="col-md-6">
        <h3>Capitalize</h3>
        <p class="text-capitalize">
          Lorem ipsum dolor ... consequat.
        </p>
      </div>
    </div>
  </div>
  <div class="col-md-3">
    <h3>Strong and italic</h3>
    <p>
      <strong>Lorem ipsum</strong> dolor ... <em>consequat</em>.
    </p>
  </div>
</div>
```

Pay attention to the last column, where we are using the `<strong>` tags to make the text bold and the `<em>` tag to make the text italic. Refresh your web browser and see the result, like this:

Lowercase	Uppercase	Capitalize	Strong and italic
lorem ipsum dolor sit amet, consectetur adipiscing elit, sed do eiusmod tempor incididunt ut labore et dolore magna aliqua. ut enim ad minim veniam, quis nostrud exercitation ullamco laboris nisi ut aliquip ex ea commodo consequat	LOREM IPSUM DOLOR SIT AMET, CONSECTETUR ADIPISCING ELIT, SED DO EIUSMOD TEMPOR INCIDIDUNT UT LABORE ET DOLORE MAGNA ALIQUA. UT ENIM AD MINIM VENIAM, QUIS NOSTRUD EXERCITATION UT LAMCO LABORIS NISI UT ALIQUIP EX EA COMMODO CONSEQUAT	Lorem Ipsum Dolor Sit Amet, Consectetur Adipiscing Elit, Sed Do Eiusmod Tempor Incididunt Ut Labore Et Dolore Magna Aliqua. Ut Enim Ad Minim Veniam, Quis Nostrud Exercitation Ullamco Laboris Nisi Ut Aliquip Ex Ea Commodo Consequat	**Lorem ipsum** dolor sit amet, consectetur adipiscing elit, sed do eiusmod tempor incididunt ut labore et dolore magna aliqua. Ut enim ad minim veniam, quis nostrud exercitation ullamco laboris nisi ut aliquip ex ea commodo consequat

> **Alternative usage of bold and italic elements**
>
> You can use the `<b>` and `<i>` tags to make the text bold and italic, respectively. Although, in HTML5 the `<b>` tag is now used to stylistically offset, such keywords in paragraphs and the `<i>` tag are used for alternate voice markup.

Finally, we are going through the footer, which is the last row. If you take a look at the full layout image (the one presented at the beginning of this section), you will notice that it is composed of three columns. The first column contains a logo image, the middle one contains an inline list, and the last one has the company's contact address.

For the first column, we should just create an `<img>` tag with the `.img-responsive` class. For the second column, the inline list, we must create a `<ul>` tag. By default, every `<li>` inside a `<ul>` has the bullets on the left-hand side. To remove them, apply the `.unstyled` Bootstrap class. Also, a `<ul>` will create the `<li>` elements as a block. In our case, we want the `<li>` to appear side by side, so we use the `.list-inline` Bootstrap class to create this effect.

To present contact information in the last column, we will use the `<address>` tag. Bootstrap offers a CSS theme for this tag; you just need to keep the formatting along with the `<br>` tags, as shown in this code:

```
<footer class="row jumbotron">
  <div class="col-md-2">
    <img src="imgs/logo.png" class="img-responsive">
  </div>
  <div class="col-md-7">
    <ul class="list-inline list-unstyled">
      <li><a href="#">Documentation</a></li>
      <li><a href="#">Packt publisher</a></li>
      <li><a href="#">Twitter</a></li>
      <li><a href="#">Bootstrap</a></li>
```

```
      <li><a href="#">Contact</a></li>
    </ul>
  </div>
  <div class="col-md-3">
    <address>
      <strong>Name, Inc.</strong><br>
      Address line 1<br>
      Address line 2<br>
      <abbr title="Phone">P:</abbr> (123) 456-7890
    </address>
  </div>
</footer>
```

Pay attention to the `<footer>` tag. We added the `.jumbotron` class to make it rounded and give it a gray background. The following screenshot presents to us the result of the footer:

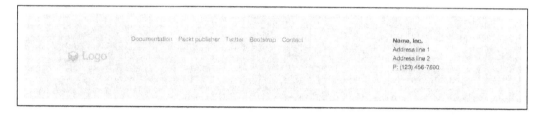

Manipulating tables

The Bootstrap framework offers a wide variety for table customization. To present them, we will create a new row before the `<footer>` and a price table for our landing page, like this:

Free plan	Standard plan	Premium plan
$ 0	$ 99	$ 999
Lorem ipsum	Lorem ipsum	Lorem ipsum
Lorem ipsum	Lorem ipsum	Lorem ipsum
Dolor sit amet	Lorem ipsum	Lorem ipsum
	Dolor sit amet	Lorem ipsum
		Lorem ipsum
Purchase	Purchase	Purchase

To do this, we must create a regular table with the `<table>`, `<thead>`, `<tbody>`, `<tr>`, `<th>`, and `<td>` tags. The table will have three columns and eight rows. Therefore, the HTML code should be like this:

```
<div class="row">
  <div class="col-md-10 col-md-offset-1">
    <table>
      <thead>
        <tr>
          <th>
            <h4>Free plan</h4>
          </th>
          <th>
            <h4>Standard plan</h4>
          </th>
          <th>
            <h4>Premium plan</h4>
          </th>
        </tr>
      </thead>
      <tbody>
        <tr>
          <td>
            <h3>$ 0</h3>
          </td>
          <td>
            <h3>$ 99</h3>
          </td>
          <td>
            <h3>$ 999</h3>
          </td>
        </tr>
        <tr>
          <td>Lorem ipsum</td>
          <td>Lorem ipsum</td>
          <td>Lorem ipsum</td>
        </tr>
        <tr>
          <td>Lorem ipsum</td>
          <td>Lorem ipsum</td>
          <td>Lorem ipsum</td>
        </tr>
        <tr>
          <td>Dolor sit amet</td>
```

```
      <td>Lorem ipsum</td>
      <td>Lorem ipsum</td>
    </tr>
    <tr>
      <td>-</td>
      <td>Dolor sit amet</td>
      <td>Lorem ipsum</td>
    </tr>
    <tr>
      <td>-</td>
      <td>-</td>
      <td>Lorem ipsum</td>
    </tr>
    <tr>
      <td><a href="#">Purchase</a></td>
      <td><a href="#">Purchase</a></td>
      <td><a href="#">Purchase</a></td>
    </tr>
  </tbody>
</table>
</div>
</div>
```

Right now, we have no secrets in our table. Let's start using CSS Bootstrap styles! First of all, add the `.table` class to the `<table>` tag (duh!). This seems redundant, but it's an option of the framework used to make it explicit.

Then, we will apply some specific styles. To make the rows striped, we add the `.table-striped` class to `<table>` as well. We want this table to have borders, so we add the `.table-bordered` class to make it like that. Last but not least, add the `.table-hover` class to enable hover state in the `<tbody>` rows.

Now we will move on to the `<tr>` tag inside `<thead>`. To make its background green, we add the `.success` class. Similar to buttons, every cell, row, or table in a `<table>` tag can receive color classes, officially called Bootstrap contextual classes.

Contextual classes follow the same colors meant for buttons. So, for the second column, we apply the `.info` class to get a cyan background color, and we use a `.danger` class to get a red background color in the last column.

 The framework also offers the `.active` class, which offers the same color of hover and the `.warning` class, which offers a yellow color.

Inside each `<th>` tag, we have an `<h4>` typography tag. If you take a look at the image showing how the table should look, you will notice that the heading texts are in the center. You may remember how to do that; just apply the `.text-center` class in the headings.

The themed `<thead>` tag will be like this:

```
<thead>
  <tr>
    <th class="success">
      <h4 class="text-center">Free plan</h4>
    </th>
    <th class="info">
      <h4 class="text-center">Standard plan</h4>
    </th>
    <th class="danger">
      <h4 class="text-center">Premium plan</h4>
    </th>
  </tr>
</thead>
```

Now we will move on to the first table row in `<tbody>`, which is the price row. We just need to center `<h4>` in the same way as we did in the `<thead>` row—by adding the `.text-center` class:

```
<h3 class="text-center">$ 0</h3>
```

The next five rows have no specific style, but the last one has buttons and some tricks!

Styling the buttons

Do you remember how to apply the color theme in the buttons? You just need to follow the `<thead>` column color style, prepending `.btn-*` in the Bootstrap contextual classes. For instance, the first one will have the `.btn-success` class to turn a green button.

Furthermore, the button must fill the full width of the cell. To make the button span the complete parent width, add the `.btn-block` class and the magic is completely done! The code for the last row is as follows:

```
<tr>
  <td><a href="#" class="btn btn-success btn-block">Purchase</a></td>
  <td><a href="#" class="btn btn-info btn-block">Purchase</a></td>
  <td><a href="#" class="btn btn-danger btn-block">Purchase</a></td>
</tr>
```

Like a boss!

Right now, we have finished the first version of our landing page! It should look like what is shown in the next screenshot. Note that we did it without a single line of custom CSS!:

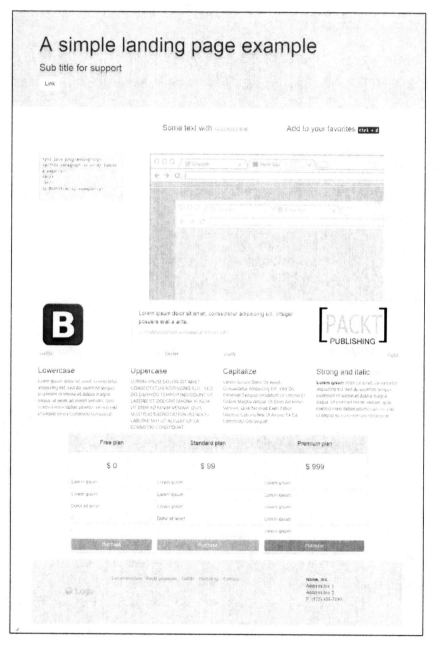

This is the power of Bootstrap. Can you feel it? You can do beautiful things very quickly. Bootstrap is a must-have tool for prototyping!

Change the viewport of your page by resizing the window and you will see how nicely Bootstrap adapts to any resolution. You don't have to worry about it if you have done a great job at making the grid and placing the elements.

Final thoughts

Before ending this chapter, we must get some things clear. Bootstrap offers some helper classes mixins and some vendor's mixins, which offer cross-browser compatibility support.

Box-sizing

Bootstrap 3 started using `box-sizing: border-box` for all elements and pseudo-elements. With this enabled, the width and height properties start to include the padding and the border but not the margin.

With that, it is easier to set the right sizing for your elements. This is because any change that you make in the element, such as customizing the padding of a `.row`, will reflect the width and height of the whole element. The following figure shows you the differences of box-sizing.

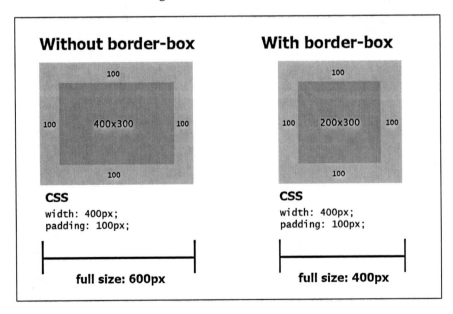

Pseudo-elements are the text placed after the : sign in the CSS style. They are used to style specific parts of elements, such as :after and :before, which are the most common pseudo-elements.

Quick floats

Bootstrap offers quick classes to make an element float. Add the .pull-left or .pull-right class to make the elements float left or right, respectively. Keep in mind that both classes apply the !important modifier to avoid override issues:

```
<div class="pull-left"></div>
<div class="pull-right"></div>
```

 In the next chapters, we will present the navbar components. Remember that if you want to align an element inside a navbar, you should use .navbar-left and .navbar-right instead of .pull-left and .pull-right.

Clearfix

Clearfix is a way of clearing the floating of an element related to its child element. The Bootstrap columns are all floated left, and the parent row has a clearfix. This makes every column appear right next to each other, and the row does not overlap with other rows. This figure exemplifies how clearfix works:

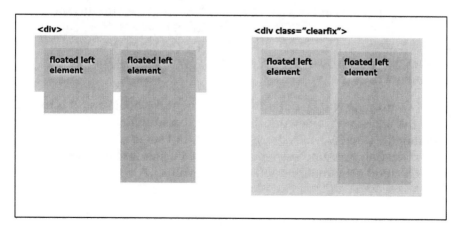

So, if you want to add the clearfix to a new element or pseudo-element, add the .clearfix class and you can get the hard work quickly done.

Font definitions for typography

In the following table, the font sizes for default text and heading are presented. It describes the heading, font family, and line height. It is important to make it explicit for you to deeply understand the Bootstrap default configuration if you want a different customization.

CSS option	Default value
font-family	"Helvetica Neue", Helvetica, Arial, and sans-serif
line-height	1.42857143 (almost 20 px)
font-size	14 px (0.875 em)
h1 font-size	36 px (2.25 em)
h2 font-size	30 px (1.875 em)
h3 font-size	24 px (1.5 em)
h4 font-size	18 px (1.125 em)
h5 font-size	14 px (0.875 em)
h6 font-size	12 px (0.75 em)
Heading line-height	16 px (1 em)

Summary

In this chapter, we started our example of creating a landing page. By now, we can create a beautiful page without a single line of CSS or JavaScript!

First, we were able to reveal the secrets behind Bootstrap's scaffolding and understand its proper usage. You learned how to set rows inside a container, columns inside rows, and settings classes for a specific viewport. We played some tricks on columns as well, making nested rows, offsetting columns, and using multiple containers.

The basis of scaffolding will be important throughout the book, and it is in fact the basis of the Bootstrap framework. The power to manipulate it is a key factor in understanding the framework. I advise you to try out some new combinations of rows in your landing page and see what happens. Further in this book, we will show you some other grid combinations and custom layouts.

Furthermore, we played with buttons, which is another key factor in Bootstrap. We presented some of the basis of button configurations and customizations. During the rest of this book, some more options will be presented in many different ways, but respecting the basis that you have just learned.

Tables are also a very common element in web pages, and Bootstrap offers a wide variety of customizations for them. We showed an example with all the main table features that you can for sure use in your daily tasks.

Finally, we saw some tricks of the framework. As I already said, you must understand the roots of Bootstrap to understand the magic. In an easy way, Bootstrap offers helpers to make our work as fast as it can get.

In the next chapter, we will dive into mobile-first development and different viewport configurations, making our landing page best fit for any device. We will also show a nice way to debug our page for any virtual devices.

3
Yes, You Should Go Mobile First

You should be asking yourself, "I thought that we should first do the layout in mobile and then go to the desktop version. Why are we in the opposing way?"

Sorry, you are right! We should always go mobile-first. We went the opposite direction just for learning purposes and now we are going to fix it.

In the current chapter, we will focus on mobile design and site responsiveness with the help of the Bootstrap framework by learning how to change the page layout for different viewport, changing the content, and more. The key points of the chapter are as follows:

- Mobile-first development
- Debugging for any device
- Bootstrap grid system for different resolutions

To figure out what, we will continue with the landing page that we developed in the last chapter.

Making it greater

Maybe you have asked yourself (or even searched for) the reason for the mobile-first paradigm trend. It is simple and makes complete sense for speeding up your development.

The main argument for the mobile-first paradigm is that it is easier to make it than to shrink it. In other words, if you make a desktop version of the web page (known as responsive design or mobile last) first and then adjust the website for mobile, it has a 99 percent probability of breaking the layout at some point and you will have to fix a lot of things.

On the other hand, if you create the mobile version first, naturally the website will use (or show) less content than the desktop version. So, it will be easier to just add the content, place the things in the right places, and create the fully responsiveness stack.

The following figure tries to illustrate this concept. Going mobile last, you will get a degraded, sharped, and crappy layout and you will get a progressively enhanced, future-friendly, awesome web page if you go mobile first. The following figure tries to illustrate the design flow of each paradigm. You can see what happens to the poor elephant... Mobile-first naturally grows the elephant instead of adjusting it:

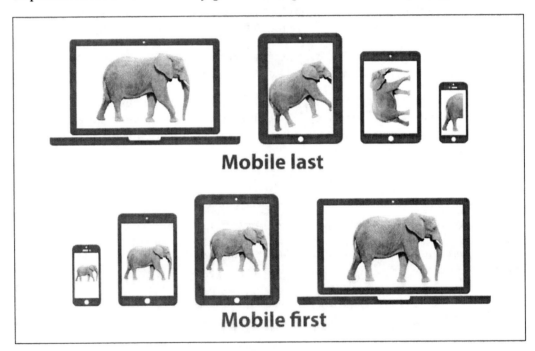

Bootstrap and the mobile-first design

In the beginning of Bootstrap, there was no concept of mobile-first. It was first used for responsive design web pages. With the Version 3 of the framework, the concept of mobile-first became very solid in the community.

The whole code of the scaffolding system was rewritten to become mobile-first from the start. They decided to reformulate how to set the grid instead of just adding mobile styles. This made a great impact in compatibility between versions older than v3, but was crucial for making the framework even more popular.

As we saw in the first chapter, to ensure the proper rendering of the page, set the correct viewport at the `<head>` tag:

```
<meta name="viewport" content="width=device-width, initial-scale=1">
```

How to debug different viewports at the browser

Let's see how to debug different viewports using the Google Chrome web browser. Even if you already know that you can skip this section, it is important to refresh the steps for doing that.

First of all, open the current landing page project that we will continue working with in this chapter in the Google Chrome browser. In the page, you need to select the **Developer tools** option. There are many ways to open this menu:

- Right-click at any place on the page and click on the last option Element inspector
- Go to the setting (the sandwich button at the top-right of the address bar), click on **More tools**, and select **Developer tools**
- The shortcut to open it is *Ctrl + Shift + I* (*cmd* for OS X users)
- *F12* in Windows also works (this is an Internet Explorer legacy)

In the **Developer tools**, click in the mobile phone on the left of a magnifier, as shown in the following screenshot:

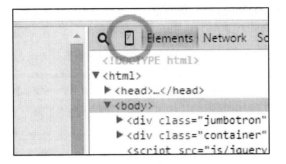

It will change the display of the viewport to a certain device and you can also set a specific network usage to limit the data bandwidth. Chrome will show a message telling you that for properly visualization you may need to reload the page to get the correct rendering.

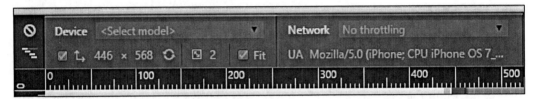

As shown in the next screenshot, we have activated the **Device** mode for an iPhone 5 device. When we set this viewport, problems started appearing because we did not make the landing page with mobile-first methodology.

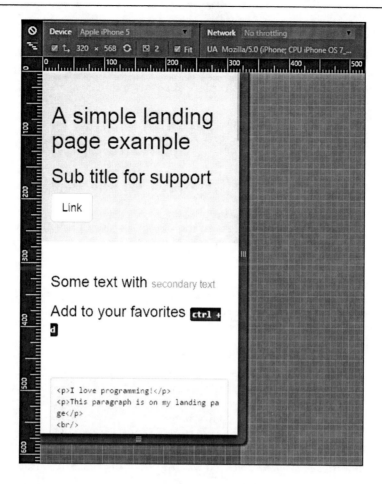

The first problem is in the second row of our layout. See how *Ctrl + D* breaks to a new line. That is not supposed to happen.

Another problem is that we have a horizontal scroll for this device due to some unknown reason. That sucks! We will have more work than with the opposite direction that starts with the mobile page. Keep it as a lesson for not repeating the same mistake.

Now, we can debug our website in different devices with different resolutions. You may see that the mouse cursor has changed to a gray circle. Also, the click actions have changed to tap actions. With that, you can fully test the website without the physical device.

Let's first clean out the messy parts in the layout before playing some tricks with the mobile version.

Cleaning up the mess

First, we will stop the line from breaking in the *Ctrl + D* text in the second row of our design. For fixing this issue, we will create our first line of CSS code. Add the <head> tag to a custom CSS file. Remember to place it below the bootstrap.css import line:

```
<link rel="stylesheet" href="css/base.css">
```

In the base.css file, create a helper class rule for .nowrap:

```
.nowrap {
    white-space: nowrap;
}
```

In the HTML file, add the created class to the <kbd> element (line 43):

```
<kbd class="nowrap"><kbd>ctrl</kbd> + <kbd>d</kbd></kbd>
```

Reload the page and you'll see that one problem is solved. Now, let's fix the horizontal scroll. Can you figure out what is making the unintended horizontal scroll? A tip, the problem is in the table!

> **What is the meaning of the white-space CSS property?**
>
> The white-space property specifies how whitespace is handled inside an element. The default is normal, where the line breaks will occur when needed. nowrap will prevent line break by creating a new line and pre will only wrap on line breaks.

The problem is caused by the buttons with the display block that make the content of each column larger than intended. To fix this, we will create our first CSS media query:

```
@media (max-width: 48em) {
    table .btn {
        font-size: 0.75rem;
        font-size: 3.5vw;
    }
}
```

Breaking down each line, first we see the current media query. The rule is that for max-width of 48em (defined in Bootstrap as small devices), apply the following rules. If the view port is greater than 48em, the rule will not be applied.

For the `.btn` elements inside the `table` element, we changed the font size (this was causing the horizontal overflow). We used a new way to set the font size based on the viewport with the `3.5vw` value. Each `1vw` corresponds to 1 percent of the total viewport. If we change the viewport, we will change the font size dynamically without breaking the layout.

Since it is a new property, nowadays just Chrome 20-34 and Safari 6 or higher have this rendering feature. For this reason, we added the other line with `font-size: 0.75rem` as a fallback case. If the browser can't handle the viewport font size, it will already had decreased the font to `12px`, which is a font that does not break the layout.

Creating the landing page for different devices

Now that we have fixed everything and learned some things about media queries and CSS3 properties, let's play with our layout and change it a bit for different devices. We will be starting with mobile and go further until we reach large desktops.

To do so, we must apply the column class for the specific viewport, as we did for medium displays using the `.col-md-*` class. The following table was presented in the previous chapter to show the different classes and the resolutions applicable for specific classes:

	Extra small devices (phones < 544px / 34em)	Small devices (tablets ≥ 544px / 34em and < 768px / 48em)	Medium devices (desktops ≥ 768px /48em < 900px / 62em)	Large devices (desktops ≥ 900px / 62em < 1200px 75em)	Extra-large devices (Desktops ≥ 1200px / 75em)
Grid behavior	Horizontal lines at all times	Collapse at start and fit column grid			
Container fixed width	Auto	544px or 34rem	750px or 45rem	970px or 60rem	1170px or 72.25rem
Class prefix	`.col-xs-*`	`.col-sm-*`	`.col-md-*`	`.col-lg-*`	`.col-xl-*`
Number of columns	12 columns				
Column fixed width	Auto	~ 44px or 2.75rem	~ 62px or 3.86rem	~ 81px or 5.06rem	~ 97px or 6.06rem

Mobile and extra small devices

To adapt our landing page to mobile devices, we will be using the Chrome mobile debug tool with the device iPhone 5 set and no network throttling.

You might have noticed that for small devices, Bootstrap just stacks each column without the referring for different rows. Some of our rows seem fine in this new grid, like the header and the second one. In the third row, it is a bit strange that the portion of code and the image are not in the same line, as shown in the following screenshot:

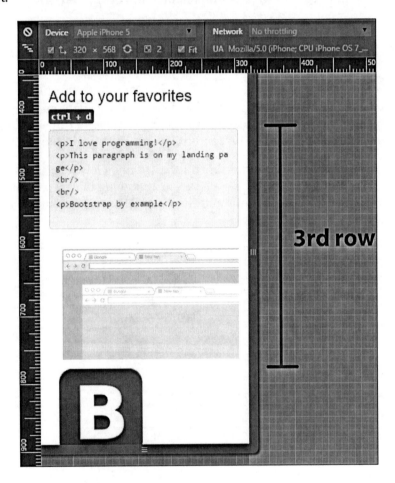

For doing that, we need to add the class columns prefix for extra small devices, which is .col-xs-*, where * is the size of the row from 1 to 12. Add the class .col-xs-5 and .col-xs-7 for the columns of the respective row (near line 49). Refresh the page and you will see now how the columns are side-by-side. The code is as follows:

```
<div class="row">
  <!-- row 3 -->
  <div class="col-md-3 col-xs-5">
    <pre>&lt;p&gt;I love programming!&lt;/p&gt;
&lt;p&gt;This paragraph is on my landing page&lt;/p&gt;
&lt;br/&gt;
&lt;br/&gt;
&lt;p&gt;Bootstrap by example&lt;/p&gt;
    </pre>
  </div>
  <div class="col-md-9 col-xs-7">
    <img src="imgs/center.png" class="img-responsive">
  </div>
</div>
```

Although the image of the web browser is too small on the right, it would be better if it was a more vertical stretched image, such a mobile phone (what a coincidence!). To make it, we need to hide the browser image in extra small devices and display an image of a mobile device. Add the new mobile image below the old one, as shown in the code:

```
<img src="imgs/mobile.png" class="img-responsive">
```

You will see both images stacked up vertically in the right column. Then, we need to use a new concept of availability classes. We need to hide the browser image and display the mobile image just for this kind of viewport, which is extra small. For that, add the class .hidden-xs in the browser image and add the class .visible-xs in the mobile image:

```
<div class="row">
  <!-- row 3 -->
  <div class="col-md-3 col-xs-5">
    <pre>&lt;p&gt;I love programming!&lt;/p&gt;
&lt;p&gt;This paragraph is on my landing page&lt;/p&gt;
&lt;br/&gt;
&lt;br/&gt;
&lt;p&gt;Bootstrap by example&lt;/p&gt;
    </pre>
```

```
      </div>
      <div class="col-md-9 col-xs-7">
        <img src="imgs/center.png" class="img-responsive hidden-xs">
        <img src="imgs/mobile.png" class="img-responsive visible-xs">
      </div>
    </div>
```

Now this row seems nice! The browser image was hidden in extra small devices and the mobile image is shown only for this viewport in question. The following screenshot shows the final display of this row:

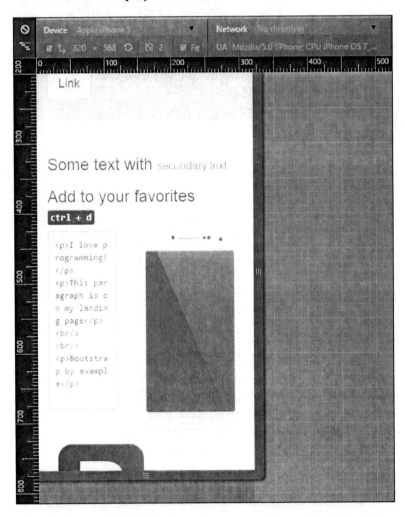

Moving on to the next row, the fourth one, it is the testimonial row surrounded by two images. It would be nicer if the testimonial appeared first and both of the images were displayed after it, splitting the same row. For this, we will repeat almost the same techniques presented in the previous row. Let's do it again for practice.

The first change is to hide the Bootstrap image with the class `.hidden-xs`. After that, create another image tag with the Bootstrap image in the same column of the PACKT image. The final code of the row should be like this:

```
<div class="row">
  <!-- row 4 -->
  <div class="col-md-3 hidden-xs">
    <img src="imgs/bs.png" class="img-responsive">
  </div>
  <div class="col-md-6 col-xs-offset-1 col-xs-11">
    <blockquote>
      <p>Lorem ipsum dolor sit amet, consectetur adipiscing elit.
Integer posuere erat a ante.</p>
      <footer>Testimonial from someone at <cite title="Source
Title">Source Title</cite></footer>
    </blockquote>
  </div>
  <div class="col-md-3 col-xs-7">
    <img src="imgs/packt.png" class="img-responsive">
  </div>
  <div class="col-xs-5 visible-xs">
    <img src="imgs/bs.png" class="img-responsive">
  </div>
</div>
```

We made plenty of things now and they are highlighted in bold. First is the `.hidden-xs` in the first column of Bootstrap image, which hid the column for this viewport.

Afterwards, in the testimonial, we changed the grid for mobile, adding a column offset with size 1 and making the testimonial fill the rest of the row with the class `.col-xs-11`.

Finally, as we said, we want to split in the same row both images from PACKT and Bootstrap. For that, make the first image column fill seven columns with the class `.col-xs-7`.

The other image column is a little more complicated. Since it is just visible for mobile devices, we add the class `.col-xs-5`. This will make the element span five columns in extra small devices. Moreover, we hide the column for other viewports with the class `.visible-xs`.

As we can see, this row has more than 12 columns (1 offset, 11 testimonial, 7 PACKT image, 5 Bootstrap image). This process is called column wrapping, and it happens when you put more than 12 columns in the same row so the groups of extra columns will wrap to the next lines.

Availability classes

Just like the `.hidden-*`, there are the `.visible-*-*` classes for each variation of display and column from 1 to 12. There is also a way to change the display CSS property using the class `.visible-*-*`, where the last `*` means block, inline, or inline-block. Use this to set the properly visualization for different visualizations.

The following screenshot shows the result of the changes. As you can see, we made the testimonial appears first, with one column of offset and both images appearing below it:

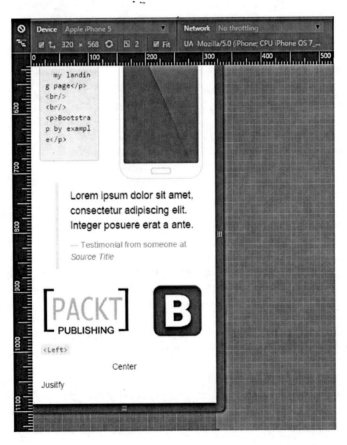

Tablets and small devices

After completing the mobile visualizations, let's go further to tablets and small devices, which are devices from 48em to 62em. Most of this these devices are tablets or old desktop monitors. For this example, we are using the iPad Mini in the portrait position with a resolution of 768 x 1024 pixels.

For this resolution, Bootstrap handles the rows just like extra small devices by just stacking up each one of the columns, making them fill the total width of the page. So if we do not want that to happen, we have to manually set the column fill for each element with the class `.col-sm-*`.

If you see how our example is presented now, there are two main problems. The first one is the second row, where the headings are in separated lines when they could be in the same. So, we just need to apply the grid classes for small devices with the class `.col-sm-6` for each column, splitting them into equal sizes:

```
<div class="row">
  <div class="col-md-offset-4 col-md-4 col-sm-6">
    <h3>
      Some text with <small>secondary text</small>
    </h3>
  </div>
  <div class="col-md-4 col-sm-6">
    <h3>
      Add to your favorites
      <small>
        <kbd class="nowrap"><kbd>ctrl</kbd> + <kbd>d</kbd></kbd>
      </small>
    </h3>
  </div>
</div>
```

The result should be as shown in the following screenshot:

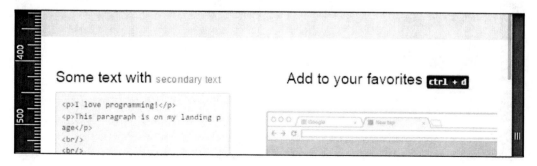

The second problem in this viewport is again the testimonial row! Because of the classes that we have added for mobile viewport, now the testimonial has an offset column and different column span. We must add the classes for small devices and make this row with the Bootstrap image on the left, the testimonial in the middle, and the PACKT image at the right position:

```
<div class="row">
  <div class="col-md-3 hidden-xs col-sm-3">
    <img src="imgs/bs.png" class="img-responsive">
  </div>
  <div class="col-md-6 col-xs-offset-1 col-xs-11 col-sm-6 col-sm-
offset-0">
    <blockquote>
      <p>Lorem ipsum dolor sit amet, consectetur adipiscing elit.
Integer posuere erat a ante.</p>
      <footer>Testimonial from someone at <cite title="Source
Title">Source Title</cite></footer>
    </blockquote>
  </div>
  <div class="col-md-3 col-xs-7 col-sm-3">
    <img src="imgs/packt.png" class="img-responsive">
  </div>
  <div class="col-xs-5 hidden-sm hidden-md hidden-lg">
    <img src="imgs/bs.png" class="img-responsive">
  </div>
</div>
```

As you can see, we had to reset the column offset in the testimonial column. It happened because it kept the offset that we added for extra small devices. Moreover, we are just ensuring that the images columns had to fill just three columns. Here's the result:

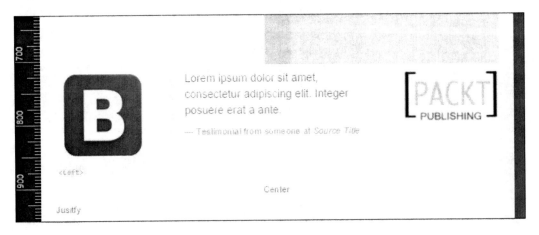

Everything else seems fine! These viewport was easier to setup. See how Bootstrap helps us a lot? Let's move to the final viewport: desktop or large devices.

Desktop and large devices

Last but not least, we enter the grid layout for desktop and large devices. We skipped medium devices, because we first coded for that viewport.

Deactivate the *device mode* in Chrome and put your page in a viewport with a width larger or equal to 1200 pixels or 75em.

The grid prefix that we will be using is `.col-lg-*`. If you take a look at the landing page, you will see that everything is well placed and we don't need to make changes! However, we would like to make some tweaks to make our layout fancier and learn some stuffs of Bootstrap grid.

We want to touch upon column ordering. It is possible to change the order of column in the same row by applying the classes `.col-lg-push-*` and `.col-lg-pull-*` (note that we are using the large devices prefix, but any other grid class prefix can be used).

The `.col-lg-push-*` means that the column will be pushed to the right by the `*` columns, where `*` is the number of columns pushed. On the other hand, `.col-lg-pull-*` will pull the column in the left direction by `*`, where `*` is the number of columns as well. Let's test this trick in the second row by changing the order of the both columns:

```
<div class="row">
  <div class="col-md-offset-4 col-md-4 col-sm-6 col-lg-push-4">
    <h3>
      Some text with <small>secondary text</small>
    </h3>
  </div>
  <div class="col-md-4 col-sm-6 col-lg-pull-4">
    <h3>
      Add to your favorites
      <small>
        <kbd class="nowrap"><kbd>ctrl</kbd> + <kbd>d</kbd></kbd>
      </small>
    </h3>
  </div>
</div>
```

We just added the class `.col-lg-push-4` to the first column and `.col-lg-pull-4` to the other one to get this result. By doing this, we changed the order of both columns in second row, as shown in the following screenshot:

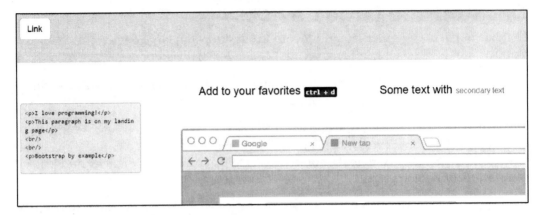

Summary

We have completed another chapter. Here, we discussed why we should always go mobile-first if we want to make a web page for every viewport, from mobile to large desktop. Making things bigger is always easier and causes less issues, so start small with mobile devices and evolve the web page until it reaches large desktop resolutions.

We saw how to debug different devices using our browser and set the right classes for each viewport. We now have our example of landing page with full stack responsiveness, working well in any device.

We covered the grid options for various devices resolutions using the mobile-first methodology—starting with mobile and going further until the large desktop version.

The main lesson of this chapter was that we always should go mobile-first. We did not follow this approach at first and because of that, we faced some problems that we could have eliminated if we had started mobile-first.

It was not mentioned before, but going mobile-first helps the whole team. The designer will have a bigger picture of what he or she needs to reach and what information is important from the beginning. The backend developer can focus on the main features and optimize them for mobile before moving on to the rest of the page content delivery. Mobile-first is also part of the development strategy.

At this point, we have our landing page fully set at all resolutions. Using Bootstrap, we took a shortcut towards responsivity, doing all the groundwork with a few lines of code in HTML and some more in CSS.

In the next chapter, we will apply some customizable styles to make the page a little less like a Bootstrap page. We will also see how to create landing pages for different uses by customizing the components.

Applying the Bootstrap Style

After making our landing page mobile-first and fully responsive for any device, it is time to go further into the Bootstrap framework, adding more and more components along with the style improvement.

This is the main objective of this chapter. We will take a step forward in terms of layout improvement, taking in regards the use of Bootstrap components. The chapter's key points are:

- Layout improvement
- Bootstrap forms
- Using images in Bootstrap
- Bootstrap helpers

By the end of this chapter, our landing page will almost be done, and you will be able to handle every HTML component customized by Bootstrap.

Changing our grid layout

First of all, the grid that we used for the current landing page is just a showcase of Bootstrap's potential and possibilities of customization. In this chapter, our objective is to make the grid fancier and more beautiful. To do this, we will change the grid to be like the one presented in the next figure.

We will go a little faster this time, since you already know how to create the grid using Bootstrap. Also, we will go mobile-first, as we discussed in the last chapter, but the screenshots will be taken from larger viewports just to improve the understandability.

1	**Company name** About Features Pricing Contact
2	**Company name** **Headline message** social button social button
3	Image **Headline** Text content **Headline** Text content Image
4	**Features** Features headline message Feature 1 Feature 2 Feature 3 Feature 4 Feature 5 Feature 6
5	**Price table**
6	**Contact info**

Starting over the grid system

As you can see in the grid image, we split the grid into six parts. This time, each part will be a section that we will present step by step. If you are starting the example from scratch, don't forget to keep the boilerplate that we presented previously.

The header

So, we will start with the header. The code for representing the grid presented should be this one, to be placed right after the `<body>` tag:

```
<header>
  <div class="container">
    <!-- row 1 -->
    <div class="row">
      <a class="brand pull-left" href="#">Company name</a>
      <ul class="list-inline list-unstyled pull-right">
        <li><a href="#about">About</a></li>
        <li><a href="#features">Features</a></li>
        <li><a href="#pricing">Pricing</a></li>
        <li><a href="#contact">Contact</a></li>
      </ul>
    </div>
  </div>
</header>
```

As you can see, the `<header>` tag is wrapping all of our `.container`, making it similar to a section. Just for the note, to have the brand link placed on the left-hand side and the list on the right-hand side, we added the `.pull-left` and `.pull-right` classes to it, respectively. These are two Bootstrap helpers.

Now, let's modify our CSS to change the header style. Remember to import the custom CSS file at `<header>`:

```
<link rel="stylesheet" href="css/base.css">
```

For that part, we will change the background color and the alignment to a better placement of the link and list elements, so let's customize and override some styles from Bootstrap:

```
header {
  background-color: #F8F8F8;
}

header ul {
```

```
      margin: 0;
    }

    header a,
    header li {
      padding: 1.4rem 0;
      color: #777;
      font-weight: bold;
    }
```

The header will look like what is shown in the following screenshot:

Company name		About	Features	Pricing	Contact

The introduction header

We have called the *introduction* header *section 2* of our grid. In this section, we have a big name of the company followed by the tagline and some buttons. The code for this row should be as follows:

```html
<section id="intro-header">
  <div class="container">
    <!-- row 2 -->
    <div class="row">
      <div class="wrap-headline">
        <h1 class="text-center">Company name</h1>
        <h2 class="text-center">Tagline message</h2>
        <hr>
        <ul class="list-inline list-unstyled text-center">
          <li>
            <a class="btn btn-default btn-lg" href="#"
role="button">Sign in</a>
          </li>
          <li>
            <a class="btn btn-primary btn-lg" href="#"
role="button">Sign up</a>
          </li>
        </ul>
      </div>
    </div>
  </div>
</section>
```

So, we have wrapped the entire container in a section, just as we said we would. There is no secret here; we used `<h1>` for the company name and `<h2>` for the tagline. We placed the buttons in a centered list, just like the headlines, using the `.text-center` helper class, and the buttons are all set as before.

We will place a big image as the background for the `#intro-header` section. To do this, we edit the CSS file as follows:

```
section#intro-header {
  background-image: url(../imgs/landscape.jpg);
  background-size: cover;
}
```

The background set as `cover` will do the trick for us to make the image cover full width, although the size of the section is too small right now. For that, we will use our `.wrap-headline` element to do the trick and make it bigger:

```
section#intro-header .wrap-headline {
  position: relative;
  padding-top: 20%;
  padding-bottom: 20%;
}
```

As you may notice, we let a `20%` padding at the top and bottom relative to our current position. With this, the height of the section becomes responsive to any viewport.

Moving on, we add some more CSS rules just for formatting, as follows:

```
section#intro-header {
  background-image: url(../imgs/landscape.jpg);
  background-size: cover;
}

section#intro-header .wrap-headline {
  position: relative;
  padding-top: 20%;
  padding-bottom: 20%;
}

section#intro-header h1,
section#intro-header h2 {
  color: #FFF;
}
```

```
section#intro-header h2 {
  font-size: 1.5rem;
}

section#intro-header hr {
  width: 10%;
}

section#intro-header .btn-default {
  background-color: rgba(255, 255, 255, 0.5);
  border: none;
}
```

The final output of those two sections should be like the one shown in the following screenshot. Pretty fancy, isn't it?

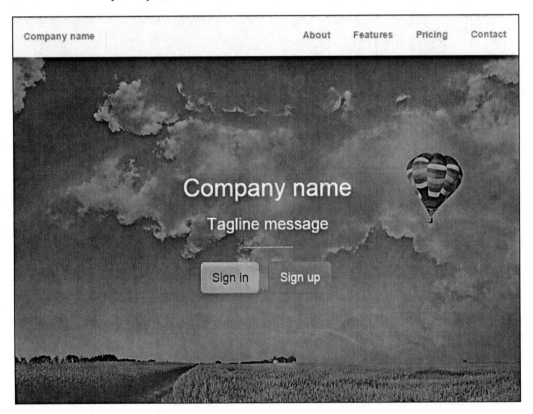

The about section

So, for the *about* section, we will place a container that wraps all of the section as well. We will play with two rows equally divided, in which we will display an image and text alternated side by side. The code for this section should be as follows:

```html
<section id="about">
  <div class="container">
    <!-- row 3 -->
    <div class="row">
      <div class="col-sm-6">
        <img src="imgs/mock_ipad.jpg" class="img-responsive">
      </div>
      <div class="col-sm-6">
        <h3>Lorem ipsum dolor sit amet</h3>
        <p>
          Lorem ipsum dolor...
        </p>
      </div>
    </div>
    <hr>

    <!-- row 4 -->
    <div class="row">
      <div class="col-sm-6">
        <h3>Lorem ipsum dolor sit amet</h3>
        <p>
          Lorem ipsum dolor...
        </p>
      </div>
      <div class="col-sm-6">
        <img src="imgs/mock_nexus.jpg" class="img-responsive">
      </div>
    </div>
  </div>
</section>
```

At this section, we just created two rows with two columns in each one. Since the columns are equally divided, they receive the `.col-sm-6` class. We added the `.img-responsive` class to the images to keep the ratio over the viewport and placed some text content on the image side of the column.

For the CSS, we add some rules to increase the margin between the content and the top portion of the page:

```
section#about img {
  margin-top: 6.5rem;
  margin-bottom: 5rem;
}

section#about h3 {
  margin-top: 10rem;
}
```

The following screenshot shows the resultant output of this section. Check whether the result of your code is similar to the following screenshot, and then let's move on to the *features* section:

The features section

The *features* section is composed of two lines of three columns, although we will create only one .row element and use the column wrapper technique. Do you remember it?

The column wrapper technique uses more than 12 parts of columns in a single row. The columns that overflow the .row will then be placed in the line below, creating the effect similar to having two .row elements:

```html
<section id="features">
  <div class="container">

    <!-- row 5 -->
    <div class="row">
      <div class="col-sm-12">
        <h3 class="text-center">Features</h3>
        <p class="text-center">Features headline message</p>
      </div>
    </div>

    <!-- row 6 -->
    <div class="row">
      <div class="col-sm-2 col-md-4">
        <div class="feature">Feature</div>
      </div>
      <div class="col-sm-2 col-md-4">
        <div class="feature">Feature</div>
      </div>
      <div class="col-sm-2 col-md-4">
        <div class="feature">Feature</div>
      </div>
      <div class="col-sm-2 col-md-4">
        <div class="feature">Feature</div>
      </div>
      <div class="col-sm-2 col-md-4">
        <div class="feature">Feature</div>
      </div>
      <div class="col-sm-2 col-md-4">
        <div class="feature">Feature</div>
      </div>
      </div>
    </div>
  </div>
</section>
```

In this section, we created two rows. The first one holds the title and headline of the section with the `<h3>` and `<p>` tags, respectively. The second row is just composed of six equal columns with the `.col-sm-2` and `.col-md-4` classes. The use of `.col-sm-2` will place the `.feature` elements in a single line when using a small viewport.

Now, edit the CSS, and let's change the text color and add some padding between the features columns list:

```css
section#features {
  background-color: #eef2f5;
  border-top: 0.1rem solid #e9e9e9;
  border-bottom: 0.1rem solid #e9e9e9;
}

section#features * {
  color: #657C8E;
}

section#features .feature {
  padding-top: 2rem;
  padding-bottom: 4rem;
  text-align: center;
}
```

The following screenshot presents the final output for the features section. Then it is time for us to start modifying the price table. It should be easy since we have already done the groundwork for it.

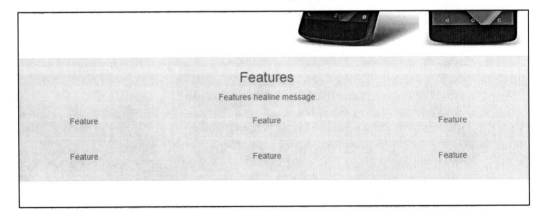

The price table section

For the *price table* section, we will use the same table from the *Manipulating tables* section in *Chapter 2, Creating a Solid Scaffolding,* but with a few modifications to make it prettier. We will make some small changes, as presented in the following code:

```html
<section id="pricing">
  <div class="container">

    <!-- row 7 -->
    <div class="row">
      <div class="col-sm-12">
        <h3 class="text-center price-headline">Price table</h3>
      </div>
    </div>

    <!-- row 8 -->
    <div class="row">
      <div class="col-sm-10 col-sm-offset-1">
        <table class="table table-striped table-hover">
          <thead>
            <tr>
              <th class="success">
                <h4 class="text-center white-text">Free plan</h4>
              </th>
              <th class="info">
                <h4 class="text-center white-text">Standard
plan</h4>
              </th>
              <th class="danger">
                <h4 class="text-center white-text">Premium
plan</h4>
              </th>
            </tr>
          </thead>
          <tbody>
            <tr>
              <td class="success">
                <h3 class="text-center white-text">$ 0</h3>
              </td>
              <td class="info">
                <h3 class="text-center white-text">$ 99</h3>
              </td>
```

```
                <td class="danger">
                  <h3 class="text-center white-text">$ 999</h3>
                </td>
              </tr>
              <tr>
                <td>Lorem ipsum</td>
                <td>Lorem ipsum</td>
                <td>Lorem ipsum</td>
              </tr>
              <tr>
                <td>Lorem ipsum</td>
                <td>Lorem ipsum</td>
                <td>Lorem ipsum</td>
              </tr>
              <tr>
                <td>Dolor sit amet</td>
                <td>Lorem ipsum</td>
                <td>Lorem ipsum</td>
              </tr>
              <tr>
                <td>-</td>
                <td>Dolor sit amet</td>
                <td>Lorem ipsum</td>
              </tr>
              <tr>
                <td>-</td>
                <td>-</td>
                <td>Lorem ipsum</td>
              </tr>
              <tr>
                <td><a href="#" class="btn btn-success btn-
block">Purchase</a></td>
                <td><a href="#" class="btn btn-info btn-
block">Purchase</a></td>
                <td><a href="#" class="btn btn-danger btn-
block">Purchase</a></td>
              </tr>
            </tbody>
          </table>
        </div>
      </div>
    </div>
</section>
```

The first change is that we added a header, `<h3>`, in this section in the first row. Furthermore, we added the `.success`, `.info`, and `.danger` classes to the first `<tr>` in `<tbody>` (they are highlighted in bold).

Also in `<table>`, we removed the `.table-bordered` class to take out the border from it. Finally, we changed some colors in the CSS file and created the `.white-text` class, which is highlighted in the code as well:

```
section#pricing h3.price-headline {
  margin-top: 5rem;
  margin-bottom: 3rem;
}

section#pricing .white-text {
  color: #FFF;
}

section#pricing thead .success {
  background-color: #78CFBF;
}

section#pricing thead .info {
  background-color: #3EC6E0;
}

section#pricing thead .danger {
  background-color: #E3536C;
}

section#pricing tbody .success {
  background-color: #82DACA;
}

section#pricing tbody .info {
  background-color: #53CFE9;
}

section#pricing tbody .danger {
  background-color: #EB6379;
}
```

The following screenshot presents the result of the price table. Finally, to sum it up, we will advance to the footer, which contains the contact information:

Price table		
Free plan	Standard plan	Premium plan
$ 0	$ 99	$ 999
Lorem ipsum	Lorem ipsum	Lorem ipsum
Lorem ipsum	Lorem ipsum	Lorem ipsum
Dolor sit amet	Lorem ipsum	Lorem ipsum
-	Dolor sit amet	Lorem ipsum
-	-	Lorem ipsum
Purchase	Purchase	Purchase

The footer

For the footer, we will have five columns, the first one being the logo with a `.col-sm-2`. This will be followed by three info columns, each one with a `.col-sm-2` as well. The last column is the address column, with the `.col-sm-4` class. The HTML code is as follows:

```
<footer>
  <div class="container">
    <div class="col-sm-2">
      <img src="imgs/logo.png" class="img-responsive">
    </div>
    <div class="col-sm-2">
      <h5>The company</h5>
      <ul class="list-unstyled">
        <li><a href="#">Documentation</a></li>
        <li><a href="#">Packt publisher</a></li>
        <li><a href="#">About us</a></li>
        <li><a href="#">Contact</a></li>
      </ul>
    </div>
```

```html
<div class="col-sm-2">
  <h5>Social</h5>
  <ul class="list-unstyled">
    <li><a href="#">Facebook</a></li>
    <li><a href="#">Twitter</a></li>
    <li><a href="#">Blog</a></li>
  </ul>
</div>
<div class="col-sm-2">
  <h5>Support</h5>
  <ul class="list-unstyled">
    <li><a href="#">Contact</a></li>
    <li><a href="#">Privacy police</a></li>
    <li><a href="#">Terms & conditions</a></li>
    <li><a href="#">Help desk</a></li>
  </ul>
</div>
<div class="col-sm-4">
  <address>
    <strong>Name, Inc.</strong>
    Address line 1<br>
    Address line 2<br>
    <abbr title="Phone">P:</abbr> (123) 456-7890
  </address>
</div>
</div>
</footer>
```

Now, let's prettify the footer with some CSS rules:

```css
footer {
  background-color: #191919;
  color: #ADADAD;
  margin-top: 3em;
}

footer h5,
footer img {
  margin-top: 5em;
  font-weight: bold;
}

footer address {
  margin-top: 5em;
```

```
    margin-bottom: 5em;
    color: #5A5A5A;
  }

footer ul {
    margin-bottom: 5em;
  }

footer address strong {
    color: #ADADAD;
    display: block;
    padding-bottom: 0.62em;
  }

footer a {
    font-weight: 300;
    color: #5A5A5A;
  }

footer a:hover {
    text-decoration: none;
    color: #FFF;
  }
```

So, we basically changed the background to a shaded one, added some margins to make the footer larger, and modified the links' colors. And we are done with the new layout! See in the following screenshot how the final layout for the footer looks:

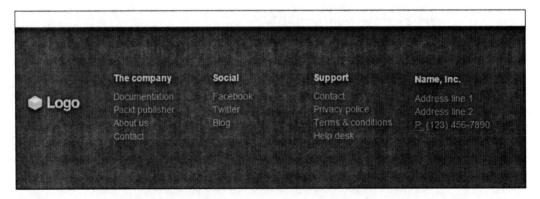

Resize the viewport and you will see how the page correctly adapts to any kind of resolution. So we have made the page again, this time with the mobile-first perspective in mind, adding more content and using Bootstrap as our backup. Nicely done!

Forming the forms

The Web would not be the same without forms. They are one of the major methods of interacting with a web page and sending data to consolidate. Since the beginning of the Web, the style and rendering of forms were a source of trouble, because they were displayed differently for each browser and there were placement problems.

This is one of the reasons Bootstrap appeared to make all web pages follow the same rendering pattern for any browser and device. For forms, this is no different. There are styles for almost every kind of element. We will start talking about forms in this section, although we will keep discussing them in later chapters as well, since they are an important element in frontend web development.

Newsletter form

To start easy, we will use an inline form in our landing page. Let's add a new row between the price table row and the footer with the following HTML code:

```
<section id="newsletter" class="text-center">
  <h4>Stay connected with us. Join the newsletter to receive fresh
info.</h4>
  <form class="form-inline" method="POST">
    <div class="form-group">
      <input class="form-control" placeholder="You name">
    </div>
    <div class="form-group">
      <input class="form-control" placeholder="Your email">
    </div>
    <button type="submit" class="btn btn-primary">Join
now!</button>
  </form>
</section>
```

OK, we're starting to break down every part of the code. The first part — we just created a new `<section>` and centralized it using the `.text-center` class from the Bootstrap helpers.

The first form type that you will learn about is `.form-inline`, which simply makes all the controls inside it the inline-block kind. Because of that, we are able to centralize the form using the `.text-center` helper. Also, this form will make the controls inline until the small viewport, when it changes the controls to become blocks, each one filling one line.

Inside .form-inline, we have two div.form-group. Every element inside a <form> that contains the .form-group class will automatically be displayed as a block element. In almost every form element, we will have a .form-group, since it is an important wrapper for labels and controls for the purpose of optimizing spacing in Bootstrap.

In our case, since we set the form to be the inline kind (because of the .form-inline class), the .form-group elements will be inline elements as well.

The two <input> are not magical; just place it in your code as shown. The same applies to the button, by using the .btn-primary class to make it blue.

The CSS for this section is quite simple. We have just made some tweaks for better rendering:

```
section#newsletter {
  border-top: 1px solid #E0E0E0;
  padding-top: 3.2em;
  margin-top: 2em;
}

section#newsletter h4 {
  padding: 1em;
}

section#newsletter form {
  padding: 1em;
  margin-top: 2em;
  margin-bottom: 5.5em;
}
```

Our first form is complete! The following screenshot shows the final output of the form:

This one was the simplest form. Now let's crack some other forms to nail it in Bootstrap.

Contact form

To make a *contact* form, we need to create another HTML file. Name it `contact.html` and use the same header and footer that you used earlier in the landing page. The final output is shown in the next image. Let's break down each part of the form to achieve the final result:

First of all, we need to create the grid for this form. As you can see, the form is in the center of the page, so to do that, create this HTML code:

```
<section id="contact" class="container">
  <div class="row">
    <div class="col-sm-offset-2 col-sm-8">
        ...
    </div>
  </div>
</section>
```

We just created the grid for this container. Inside this column, we need to create a `<form>` element with the following code:

```
<form class="form-horizontal">
  <div class="form-group">
```

```
    <label class="col-sm-2 control-label" for="contact-name">Name</
label>
    <div class="col-sm-10">
      <input class="form-control" type="text" id="contact-name"
placeholder="Full name">
    </div>
  </div>
  <div class="form-group">
    <label class="col-sm-2 control-label" for="contact-email">Email</
label>
    <div class="col-sm-10">
      <input class="form-control" type="text" id="contact-email"
placeholder="Contact email">
    </div>
  </div>
  <div class="form-group">
    <label class="col-sm-2 control-label" for="contact-
email">Message</label>
    <div class="col-sm-10">
      <textarea class="form-control" rows="3" placeholder="Type
your message"></textarea>
    </div>
  </div>
  <div class="form-group">
    <div class="col-sm-offset-2 col-sm-10">
      <label class="checkbox">
        <input type="checkbox" value="">
        I want to subscribe to receive updates from the company.
      </label>
    </div>
  </div>
  <div class="form-group">
    <div class="col-sm-offset-2 col-sm-10">
      <button class="btn btn-success btn-lg"
type="submit">Submit</button>
    </div>
  </div>
</form>
```

At first sight, it looks like a common form, with two input fields, a text area, a checkbox, and a *submit* button. The .form-horizontal class is responsible for aligning the labels and the inputs side by side horizontally. Note that we are using the .col-sm-* grid classes in both labels and inputs in a grid of 12 parts inside .form-group, just like the column nesting technique.

In the `.form-group` checkbox, we created a `<div>` with an offset of 2 to fill the part that is not needed in this case. Note that we are able to use the same grid classes to acquire the same results inside forms. To place the Bootstrap theme in the checkbox, just add the `.checkbox` class to the label wrapping the input.

We don't need much CSS in this section; just add some padding to give some space to the form:

```
section#contact form {
  padding-top: 9rem;
  padding-bottom: 3rem;
}
```

Let's start with some JavaScript

It's time to start playing with some JavaScript! Create a file named `main.js` inside the `js` folder, which also contains the Bootstrap JavaScript file and jQuery library. To do the groundwork in the JavaScript file, we need to load it after `document` is ready:

```
$(document).ready(function() {
    // document ready, place you code
});
```

Then, we will validate the form before sending it. To do that, attach an event handler to the form submission, like this:

```
$(document).ready(function() {
    $('#contact form').on('submit', function(e) {
        e.preventDefault();
    });
});
```

You may know this, but the `e.preventDefault()` code line is a method that prevents the default action from being triggered, the form submission in this case.

Moving on, we create the variables that we will use and the validation code:

```
$(document).ready(function() {
    $('#contact form').on('submit', function(e) {
        e.preventDefault();
        var $form = $(e.currentTarget),
            $email = $form.find('#contact-email'),
            $button = $form.find('button[type=submit]');

        if($email.val().indexOf('@') == -1) {
            vaca = $email.closest('form-group')
```

```
            $email.closest('.form-group').addClass('has-error');
        } else {
            $form.find('.form-group').addClass('has-success').
removeClass('has-error');
            $button.attr('disabled', 'disabled');
            $button.after('<span>Message sent. We will contact you
soon.</span>');
        }
    });
});
```

So, we first created our variables for the form, the email field, and the button element. After that, we performed a naïve validation on the email field, where if the @ character is present in the field, it is valid. If it is not present, we add the .has-error class to the parent .form-group of the field. It will produce the elements inside the form group in red, as presented in the following screenshot:

Load the JavaScript file in the HTML of contact.html just below where bootstrap.js loads:

```
<script src="js/bootstrap.js"></script>
<script src="js/main.js"></script>
```

If the @ sign is present in the field, we simply pass the validation by fake-sending it. When this happens, we add the .has-success class to each .form-group, making them green. We also add the attribute disabled to the button, changing its behavior and theme as Bootstrap does it.

Finally, we add after the button a simple feedback message for the user, saying that the contact message was sent. The following screenshot shows the case where the contact message is successfully sent:

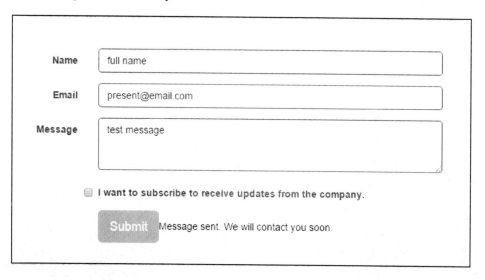

The sign-in form

Now that you have learned some more form styles in the contact file, we will play with another kind of form: the sign-in form.

Go back to the landing page HTML file, and in the sign in `.btn` located inside the introduction header, add the `#sign-btn` identifier:

```
<a id="sign-btn" class="btn btn-default btn-lg" href="#"
role="button">Sign in</a>
```

After the `<ul>` that wraps the sign buttons, place the sign-in form code:

```
<form id="signin" class="form-inline text-center hidden-element">
  <div class="form-group">
    <div class="input-group">
      <div class="input-group-addon">@</div>
      <input type="text" class="form-control" id="signin-email"
placeholder="Email">
    </div>
  </div>
  <div class="form-group">
    <div class="input-group">
      <div class="input-group-addon">*</div>
```

```
        <input type="password" class="form-control" id="signin-password"
placeholder="Password">
      </div>
    </div>
    <button type="submit" class="btn btn-default">Sign in</button>
  </form>
```

The result should be like what is shown in the following screenshot, where the new form appears after the buttons:

Before moving on to fixing the layout, let's explain `.input-group`. Bootstrap offers this option to prepend or append things to an input using `.input-group-addon`. In this case, we prepend @ and * to each input. We could also have appended this to the inputs by placing `.input-group-addon` after the input instead of before.

For the CSS, we just added the `.hidden-element` rule. We could not use the `.hidden` Bootstrap helper because it applies the `!important` option, and we would not have been able to make it visible again without removing the class:

```
.hidden-element {
  display: none;
}
```

Let's animate it a little! Go to the JavaScript file and add the event listener to the click on the sign-in button:

```
$(document).ready(function() {
    ... // rest of the JavaScript code
    $('#sign-btn').on('click', function(e) {
        $(e.currentTarget).closest('ul').hide();
        $('form#signin').fadeIn('fast');
    });
});
```

By doing this, we hide the `<ul>` element that contains the *sign* buttons and show the sign in form. That was just the cherry on our pie, and we are done with forms by now! Refresh the web page in the browser, click on the **Sign in** button, and see the new form appearing. Moving forward, we will use some images and see how Bootstrap can help us with that.

Images

For images, Bootstrap offers some classes to make your day better. We have already discussed the use of the `.img-responsive` class, on which the image becomes scalable by setting `max-width: 100%` and `height: auto`.

The framework also offers three convenient classes to style your image. To make use of that, place the following code after the price table in the landing:

```
<section id="team">
  <div class="container">
    <div class="row">
      <div class="col-sm-12">
        <ul class="list-inline list-unstyled text-center">
          <li>
            <img src="imgs/jon.png" class="img-rounded">
            <h5>Jonny Doo</h5>
            <p>CEO</p>
          </li>
          <li>
            <img src="imgs/jon.png" class="img-circle">
            <h5>Jonny Doo</h5>
            <p>CTO</p>
          </li>
          <li>
```

```
            <img src="imgs/jon.png" class="img-thumbnail">
            <h5>Jonny Doo</h5>
            <p>CIO</p>
         </li>
      </ul>
   </div>
  </div>
</section>
```

As you can notice, we simply created another container and row with a single column, .col-sm-12. Inside the column, we added an inline list with the elements, each one having one image with a different class. The .img-rounded class makes the corners rounded, .img-circle turns the image into a circular shape, and .img-thumbnail adds a nice rounded border to the image, like this:

The preceding screenshot shows how this section is displayed. We also had to add some CSS code to increase margins and paddings, along with font customization:

```
section#team ul {
   margin: 5rem 0;
}

section#team li {
   margin: 0 5rem;
}

section#team h5 {
   font-size: 1.5rem;
   font-weight: bold;
}
```

So, it's nice to have a backup of Bootstrap, even with the images, making our work easier and pacing up the development. By the way, Bootstraps offers tons of helpers with the same objective. We have already used some of them; now let's use even more.

Helpers

Helpers are Bootstrap classes that help us achieve certain customizations. They are planned to offer a single purpose and reduce CSS frequency of repeated rules. The goal is always the same: increase the pace of development.

Floating and centering blocks

We have talked previously about the `.pull-left` and `.pull-right` classes, which make the HTML element float to the left or right. To center the block, you can use the `.center-block` class.

To make use of this, go to the column that wraps the pricing table, and replace the `.col-sm-10.col-sm-offset-1` classes with `.center-block`. In the CSS, add the following rule:

```
section#pricing .center-block {
  width: 90%
}
```

Refresh the web page and you will see that the table stays centered, but now using a different approach.

Context colors

You can apply the same colors that we used in buttons and the price table to every element in the page. To do that, use these classes: `.text-primary`, `.text-success`, `.text-warning`, `.text-info`, `.text-danger`, and `.text-muted`.

In the images section that we have just made, apply the `.text-info` class to the `<h5>` elements and apply `.text-muted` in `<p>`:

```
<section id="team">
  <div class="container">
    <div class="row">
      <ul class="list-inline list-unstyled text-center">
        <li>
          <img src="imgs/jon.png" class="img-rounded">
          <h5 class="text-info">Jonny Doo</h5>
```

```
      <p class="text-muted">CEO</p>
    </li>
    <li>
      <img src="imgs/jon.png" class="img-circle">
      <h5 class="text-info">Jonny Doo</h5>
      <p class="text-muted">CTO</p>
    </li>
    <li>
      <img src="imgs/jon.png" class="img-thumbnail">
      <h5 class="text-info">Jonny Doo</h5>
      <p class="text-muted">CIO</p>
    </li>
  </ul>
</div>
</section>
```

Refresh the web page, and the headline element will be light blue and the paragraph text grey.

To make the opposite operation – changing the background to the context color – apply the .bg-* class, where you can pass one of the color options (primary, info, warning, or danger).

Spacing

In Bootstrap 4, they added new helpers for margins and padding spacing. If you are using Sass, you can set a default $spacer and every margin will work like a charm by using these classes, although the default value for the spacer is 1rem.

Next, we will present a table with the classes for margin usage. In summary, you will use the .m-*-* regex, where the first option is the location, such as top, bottom, and so on. The second option is the size of the margin. Refer to this table for a better understanding of the usage:

	Remove margin	Default margin	Medium margin (1.5 times)	Large margin (3 times)
All	.m-a-0	.m-a	.m-a-md	.m-a-lg
Top	.m-t-0	.m-t	.m-t-md	.m-t-lg
Right	.m-r-0	.m-r	.m-r-md	.m-r-lg
Bottom	.m-b-0	.m-b	.m-b-md	.m-b-lg
Left	.m-l-0	.m-l	.m-l-md	.m-l-lg
Horizontal	.m-x-0	.m-x	.m-x-md	.m-x-lg
Vertical	.m-y-0	.m-y	.m-y-md	.m-y-lg

For the padding, the classes are almost the same; just use the `.p-*-*` prefix to get the expected result. Remember that the default spacer is `1rem`, so the medium is `1.5rem` and large is `3rem`:

	Remove margin	Default padding	Medium padding (1.5 times)	Large padding (3 times)
All	`.p-a-0`	`.p-a`	`.p-a-md`	`.p-a-lg`
Top	`.p-t-0`	`.p-t`	`.p-t-md`	`.p-t-lg`
Right	`.p-r-0`	`.p-r`	`.p-r-md`	`.p-r-lg`
Bottom	`.p-b-0`	`.p-b`	`.p-b-md`	`.p-b-lg`
Left	`.p-l-0`	`.p-l`	`.p-l-md`	`.p-l-lg`
Horizontal	`.p-x-0`	`.p-x`	`.p-x-md`	`.p-x-lg`
Vertical	`.p-y-0`	`.p-y`	`.p-y-md`	`.p-y-lg`

Responsive embeds

The new version of Bootstrap 4 also allows us to make embeds responsive. So, there are classes for the `<iframe>`, `<embed>`, `<video>`, and `<object>` elements. To get the expected result, add the `.embed-responsive` class to your element:

```
<div class="embed-responsive embed-responsive-16by9">
  <iframe class="embed-responsive-item"
src="//www.youtube.com/embed/dQw4w9WgXcQ"
allowfullscreen></iframe>
</div>
```

We added the `.embed-responsive-16by9` class to make the aspect ratio of the video *16:9*. You can also use the aspect ratios *21:9* and *4:3* with the `.embed-responsive-21by9` and `.embed-responsive-4by3` classes respectively.

Summary

In this chapter, we remade our landing page by applying the Bootstrap theme and customizing it, getting a much better result in the end. Right now, we have a clean web page, developed quickly using the mobile-first paradigm.

You also started to learn the use of some forms by going through three examples, one of these being a complementary contact page. Along with forms, we started using JavaScript! We performed form validation and some simple animations on our page, with regard to the template.

Finally, we presented the Bootstrap image options and a bunch of helpers. Remember that there are more helpers than the ones shown in this chapter, but don't worry, because we will see them in the upcoming chapters.

If you think you already have a fancy landing page, we will prove to you that we can improve it even more! We will talk about it again in the next chapter, reaching icons, more forms, buttons, and navigation bars.

Congratulations! You have reached this point of the book. Brace yourself, because the next level is coming. We will take a step forward by using more complex elements and components of Bootstrap.

5
Making It Fancy

It is finally time to take our last step through the landing page example. After learning all the basics of Bootstrap, passing from side to side of the grid system, mobile-first development, and using Bootstrap HTML elements, the landing page example has come to an end. Now it is time to go a little deeper and acquire more knowledge of this beautiful framework—Bootstrap.

In this chapter, we will focus on adding components all over the landing page. We will also touch upon the `flexbox` option, present in version 4. After all has been said, our landing page will be ready for the production stage. Get ready for the key points that we will cover in this chapter:

- Glyphicon icons
- Navigation bars
- The Drop-down component
- Input grouping
- Flexbox Bootstrap usage

Using Bootstrap icons

Bootstrap is such a nice thing! It provides for us more than 250 icons ready for use and fully resizable. The icons were created from the Glyphicon Halflings set (http://glyphicons.com/). They are fully rendered as fonts, so you can customize both size and color for each one of them. To make use of that, let's see the features section on the landing page. As you can see, we let this section be a little simpler. By adding some fonts, we will get a nicer result:

```
<section id="features">
  <div class="container">
```

```
<!-- row 5 -->
<div class="row">
  <div class="col-sm-12">
    <h3 class="text-center">Features</h3>
    <p class="text-center">Features headline message</p>
  </div>
</div>

<!-- row 6 -->
<div class="row">
  <div class="col-sm-2 col-md-4">
    <div class="feature">
      <span class="glyphicon glyphicon-screenshot" aria-hidden="true"></span>
      <span class="feature-tag">Product focus</span>
    </div>
  </div>
  <div class="col-sm-2 col-md-4">
    <div class="feature">
      <span class="glyphicon glyphicon-education" aria-hidden="true"></span>
      <span class="feature-tag">Teaching as a passion</span>
    </div>
  </div>
  <div class="col-sm-2 col-md-4">
    <div class="feature">
      <span class="glyphicon glyphicon-send" aria-hidden="true"></span>
      <span class="feature-tag">Spreading knowledge</span>
    </div>
  </div>
  <div class="col-sm-2 col-md-4">
    <div class="feature">
      <span class="glyphicon glyphicon-hourglass" aria-hidden="true"></span>
      <span class="feature-tag">Save your day time</span>
    </div>
  </div>
  <div class="col-sm-2 col-md-4">
    <div class="feature">
      <span class="glyphicon glyphicon-sunglasses" aria-hidden="true"></span>
      <span class="feature-tag">Make it fancy</span>
    </div>
  </div>
```

```
        <div class="col-sm-2 col-md-4">
          <div class="feature">
            <span class="glyphicon glyphicon-heart" aria-
hidden="true"></span>
            <span class="feature-tag">Made with love</span>
          </div>
        </div>
        </div>
      </div>
    </div>
  </section>
```

So, from the beginning, here is the code of the modified features section. The bold text corresponds to the icon additions. It is pretty simple to add an icon. Just check out the options at http://getbootstrap.com/components/#glyphicons, copy the class code, and use it in an element. Note that you must add both classes, .glyphicon and .glyphicon-*.

The aria-hidden property

You may have noticed that there is a property called aria-hidden="true" present in all the icons. The reason for this is that the fonts are represented as Unicode characters, meaning they may represent words. Therefore, to prevent that accessibility, screen readers start reading those characters such as they are words, the aria-hidden attribute prevents that.

Even more, we made some changes to the CSS file, adding more rules for the current working section. Add the following style to the base.css file, located in the css folder:

```
section#features .feature {
  padding-top: 2rem;
  padding-bottom: 4rem;
  text-align: center;
}

section#features .glyphicon {
  font-size: 2rem;
}

section#features .glyphicon-heart {
  color: #E04C4C;
}
```

```
section#features .feature-tag {
  max-width: 10.7em;
  display: inline-block;
  text-align: left;
  margin-left: 1.5em;
  font-size: 1.7rem;
}
```

With this, we want to show some nice options that you can use with icons. The first one is that you can change the size of the icon by changing its font size. In our case, we set it to `font-size: 2rem`. The second one is that icons provide the option to change their color by just adding the CSS color rule. We applied it to the heart icon, because the heart must be red—`color: #E04C4C`.

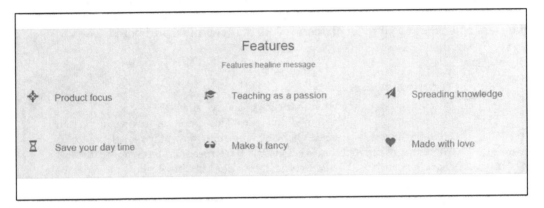

The preceding screenshot shows the final result of the **Features** section. As you can see, it is pretty simple to use icons in Bootstrap. Also, the possibilities that the framework offers are very suitable for daily adjustments, such changing icons' colors and sizes.

Using other icons sets

There are plenty of other icon sets out there that can be used just like glyphicons for Bootstrap. Among all of them, it is worth mentioning Font Awesome (`https://fortawesome.github.io/Font-Awesome/`). It stands out from others, since it was the first icon set to use font encoding, together with a wide variety of icons.

Paying attention to your navigation

Bootstrap offers a very nice navigation bar to be placed at the top of website, or even in places where you want that behavior. Let's change our header section to make it our navigation bar. It will stick to the top of the web page, working as a navigation menu.

First of all, let's use a `<nav>` element and add to it the `.navbar` and `.navbar-default` classes, which are required for the component, and the `.navbar-fixed-top` class to fix the element at the top. Replace the `<header>` HTML section with the following code:

```html
<nav class="navbar navbar-default navbar-fixed-top">
  <div class="navbar-header">
    <a class="navbar-brand" href="landing_page.html">Company name</a>
  </div>
  <div class="navbar-right">
      <ul class="nav navbar-nav">
        <li><a href="#about">About</a></li>
        <li><a href="#features">Features</a></li>
        <li><a href="#pricing">Pricing</a></li>
        <li><a href="contact.html">Contact</a></li>
      </ul>
  </div>
</nav>
```

As was mentioned, the `.navbar` and `.navbar-default` classes are required for the navigation component. For the **Company name** link, we added a class, `.navbar-brand`, which has the purpose of branding the heading with an appropriate font size and padding.

Then, we created a `<div>` tag using the `.navbar-right` class to provide a set padding CSS rules and place the list to the right to appear the same way as was before. For the CSS, just add the following rule to create a padding to the `<body>` of your page:

```css
body {
  padding-top: 3.6em;
}

#nav-menu {
  margin-right: 1rem;
}
```

The result of the navigation bar should be like what is presented in the following screenshot:

Until the navigation collapse

Try to resize the web page and you will see that for small viewports, the horizontal list placed in the navigation will stack vertically, as illustrated in the next screenshot. Fortunately, Bootstrap has the option to collapse the lists at the navigation bar. The procedure for doing this is pretty simple and we will do it now.

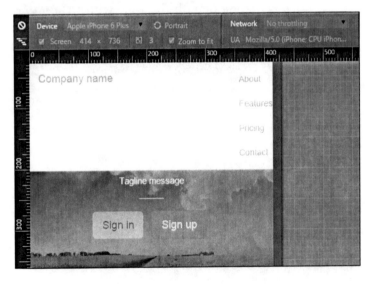

So, let's make the `.nav-header` collapses and create a `toggle` button to show or hide the list menu. Change the HTML to this:

```
<nav class="navbar navbar-default navbar-fixed-top">
  <div class="navbar-header">
    <a class="navbar-brand" href="landing_page.html">Company
name</a>
    <button type="button" class="navbar-toggle collapsed" data-
toggle="collapse" data-target="#nav-menu" aria-expanded="false">
      <span class="sr-only">Toggle navigation</span>
      <span class="icon-bar"></span>
      <span class="icon-bar"></span>
      <span class="icon-bar"></span>
    </button>
  </div>

  <div id="nav-menu" class="collapse navbar-collapse navbar-right">
      <ul class="nav navbar-nav">
        <li><a href="#about">About</a></li>
        <li><a href="#features">Features</a></li>
        <li><a href="#pricing">Pricing</a></li>
        <li><a href="contact.html">Contact</a></li>
      </ul>
  </div>
</nav>
```

The new code is in bold. First, we added a `<button>` element to create our *sandwich button* (the one with three dashes). On `data-target`, we must add the element that is the collapse target, `#nav-menu` in our case.

Then, we must say which is the element to be collapsed in the small viewport, so for `.navbar-right`, we added the `.collapse.navbar-collapse` classes. The navigation bar should then appear like the one shown in the following screenshot. Hooray! Bootstrap has saved the day again!

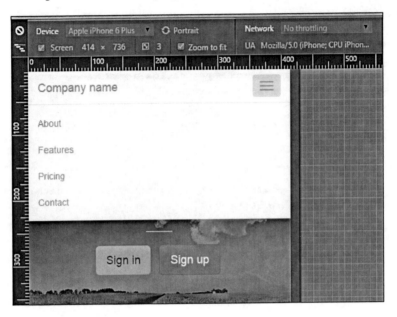

 In order to use `.navbar-collapse`, you should remember to load the Bootstrap JavaScript library as well.

Using different attachments

For this example, we fixed the navigation bar to the top of our web page, although we can use different attachments. For instance, we can attach the navigation bar to the bottom using the `.navbar-fixed-bottom` class.

 If it is attached in the bottom, do not forget to change the `<body>` padding from `top` to `bottom` in the CSS code.

The bar can also be static. For that, use the `.navbar-static-*` class, where the asterisk can mean `top` or `bottom`. If you are using the static navigation bars, you must place a container (static or fluid) right in the next level of the component:

```
<nav class="navbar navbar-default navbar-static-top">
  <div class="container">
    ...
  </div>
</nav>
```

Coloring the bar

You can also change the color of the navigation bar. Bootstrap version 3 offers an inverted set of colors. To do so, add the `.navbar-inverse` class to the `<nav>` element, as follows:

```
<nav class="navbar navbar-inverse">
  ...
</nav>
```

In version 4, they added other color options. So if the background of your navigation bar has a dark color, add the `.navbar-dark` class to make the text and other elements white. If the background has a light color, use the `.navbar-light` class to get the opposite result.

For the background color, you can pass a class called `.bg-*`, where the asterisk means a set of colors from Bootstrap. These are `default`, `primary`, `info`, `success`, `warning`, or `danger`:

```
<nav class="navbar navbar-dark bg-danger">
  ...
</nav>
```

Dropping it down

It is time to go back to the buttons once more. Now we will use the buttons dropdown. Button dropdowns are great for grouping a set of options in a single button. It can be used in several situations.

 Remember that it is necessary to use Bootstrap JavaScript for buttons drop-downs as well.

To make use of these, you just need to make some small markups and class usages. We will also go a little further and add a button dropdown to our new navigation bar. The complete HTML code of the <nav> tag is this one:

```html
<nav class="navbar navbar-default navbar-fixed-top">
  <div class="navbar-header">
    <a class="navbar-brand" href="landing_page.html">Company
name</a>
    <button type="button" class="navbar-toggle collapsed" data-
toggle="collapse" data-target="#nav-menu" aria-expanded="false">
      <span class="sr-only">Toggle navigation</span>
      <span class="icon-bar"></span>
      <span class="icon-bar"></span>
      <span class="icon-bar"></span>
    </button>
    <!-- <a class="btn btn-primary navbar-btn pull-right" href="#"
role="button">Sign up</a> -->
  </div>

  <div class="btn-group pull-right">
    <button type="button" class="btn btn-primary dropdown-toggle"
data-toggle="dropdown" aria-haspopup="true" aria-expanded="false">
      Customer area <span class="caret"></span>
    </button>
    <ul class="dropdown-menu">
      <li><a href="#">Action</a></li>
      <li><a href="#">Another action</a></li>
      <li><a href="#">Something else here</a></li>
      <li role="separator" class="divider"></li>
      <li><a href="#">Separated link</a></li>
    </ul>
  </div>

  <div id="nav-menu" class="collapse navbar-collapse navbar-right">
    <ul class="nav navbar-nav">
      <li><a href="#about">About</a></li>
      <li><a href="#features">Features</a></li>
      <li><a href="#pricing">Pricing</a></li>
      <li><a href="contact.html">Contact</a></li>
    </ul>
  </div>
</nav>
```

The highlighted code is the new one for the drop-down button. We have to create a `<button>`, followed by a list `<ul>`, all of that wrapped by a div `.btn-group`. It is a pretty strict piece of code that should be used for these components.

Regarding the CSS, we must add some spacing between the button and the list. So, the CSS for the button drop-down is as follows:

```
nav .btn-group {
  margin: 0.8rem 2rem 0 0;
}
```

The result for the button is presented in the following screenshot:

Oops! If you see the example for large devices, the new button looks pretty good, although it looks badly placed for small devices. Let's fix this with a `media` query!

```
@media (max-width: 48em){
  nav .btn-group {
    position: absolute;
    top: 0;
    right: 4em;
  }
}
```

After the fix, the output that you get should be as shown in this screenshot:

Customizing buttons dropdown

The Bootstrap buttons dropdown offers some custom options. The first one that we will discuss is the split option. To do this, you need to change your HTML a bit:

```html
<div class="btn-group pull-right">
  <button type="button" class="btn btn-primary">Customer
area</button>
  <button type="button" class="btn btn-primary dropdown-toggle" data-
toggle="dropdown" aria-haspopup="true" aria-expanded="false">
    <span class="caret"></span>
    <span class="sr-only">Toggle Dropdown</span>
  </button>
  <ul class="dropdown-menu">
    <li><a href="#">Action</a></li>
    <li><a href="#">Another action</a></li>
    <li><a href="#">Something else here</a></li>
    <li role="separator" class="divider"></li>
    <li><a href="#">Separated link</a></li>
  </ul>
</div>
```

The main difference is the bold text, where we create another button, which will be responsible for the split effect, as shown in the following screenshot:

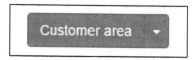

Moving on, you can make the drop-down a "drop-up". To do that, simply add the class to `div.btn-group`:

```
<div class="btn-group dropup">
  ...
</div>
```

Making an input grouping

As we discussed in the last chapter, it is possible to group components together with inputs, as we did to the sign form in the home page. However, it is possible to add even more things to inputs. We will talk about some group options that can be useful.

First of all, let's exemplify the usage of grouping inputs and buttons. The main idea is almost the same—creating a `div.input-group`, and creating an input and a button inside this element, as shown in this HTML code:

```
<div class="input-group">
  <input type="text" class="form-control" placeholder="Type the
page title...">
  <span class="input-group-btn">
    <button class="btn btn-success" type="button">Search</button>
  </span>
</div>
```

The output of the preceding code is shown in the following screenshot:

The only trick here is to add a `<span>` element wrapping the button. If you invert the input order with the button, you will prepend the button to the input:

```html
<div class="input-group">
  <span class="input-group-btn">
    <button class="btn btn-success" type="button">Search</button>
  </span>
  <input type="text" class="form-control" placeholder="Type the page
title...">
</div>
```

The output of the preceding code is shown in this screenshot:

Bootstrap also gives us the possibility to add any other kind of button. To exemplify this, let's now add a button dropdown grouped with an input. Replace `<button>` with the button dropdown that we just used in the previous example:

```html
<div class="input-group">
  <span class="input-group-btn">
    <div class="btn-group pull-right">
        <button type="button" class="btn btn-primary dropdown-toggle"
data-toggle="dropdown" aria-haspopup="true" aria-expanded="false">
          Customer area <span class="caret"></span>
        </button>
        <ul class="dropdown-menu">
          <li><a href="#">Action</a></li>
          <li><a href="#">Another action</a></li>
          <li><a href="#">Something else here</a></li>
          <li role="separator" class="divider"></li>
          <li><a href="#">Separated link</a></li>
        </ul>
    </div>
  </span>
  <input type="text" class="form-control" placeholder="Type the
page title...">
</div>
```

It is pretty simple; you can add almost any kind of button, prepended or appended in an input. The following screenshot shows the result of the previous HTML code:

Can you append two buttons?

This is a small challenge for you. Can you append two buttons to the same input? Try to append some more buttons to `.input-group` and see what happens!

Getting ready for flexbox!

In version 4 of Bootstrap, flexbox support has finally arrived! However, it is an opt-in that can be used. The first step is to understand a little bit of flexbox, just in case you don't know, and then start using it.

We will not add any other element to our landing page example, since support for flexbox just begun with Bootstrap 4. We will cover it only to clarify this new option.

Understanding flexbox

The definition of flexbox came out with the CSS3 specifications. Its main purpose is to better organize elements in a web page in a predictable manner. It can be seen as an option similar to `float` but one that offers a lot more choices, such as reordering elements and avoiding known issues of float, for example, the `clearfix` workaround.

For a hierarchical organization, first of all, you need to wrap the element of all the flex items (such as the columns inside a `.row`). It is also possible to play with the direction and axis from the wrapping element.

To exemplify the usage, let's create an HTML example. Create another file, named flexbox.html, use your base template and place the HTML code inside the <body> tag:

```
<body>
  <div class="wrapping-flex">
    <div class="item1">Item 1</div>
    <div class="item2">Item 2</div>
    <div class="item3">Item 3</div>
  </div>
</body>
```

So, in this case, we must make the div.wrapping-flex the flex wrapping element. Apply the following CSS and you will get the child elements placed inline:

```
.wrapping-flex {
  display: -webkit-flex;
  display: flex;
  background-color: #CCC;
}

.wrapping-flex > div {
  background-color: #ECA45A;
  margin: 1rem;
  padding: 1.5rem;
}
```

Create this is a sample HTML page and you will get the following output:

There are a plenty of options for flexbox. I do recommend the guide at https:// css-tricks.com/snippets/css/a-guide-to-flexbox/ for you to learn more about flexbox, since it is not our focus.

However, let's show a very powerful use case of flexbox. Have you ever faced a problem with aligning one div inside another vertically? I hope not, because it can be a pain in the neck, even more if you made it for older browsers.

With flexbox, we just have to apply the following CSS:

```
.wrapping-flex {
  display: -webkit-flex;
  display: flex;
  background-color: #CCC;
  height: 12rem;
  width: 50%;
  margin-left: 20%;
}

.wrapping-flex > div {
  background-color: #ECA45A;
  margin: 1rem;
  padding: 1.5rem;
}

.wrapping-flex .item2 {
  align-self: center;
  height: 5rem;
}
```

We added a `height: 12rem` to the wrapping element and set `align-self: center` and `height: 5rem` to the `.item2` element. With that, we align the second flex child `<div>` in the center, while the other two children continue to occupy the full height, as shown in the following screenshot:

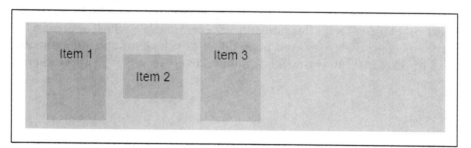

Playing with Bootstrap and flexbox

Version 4 of Bootstrap provides two ways to use flexbox. The first one is with Sass, where you need to set the `$enable-flex` variable to the `true` state.

The other option is to download the compiled CSS version using the flex opt-in. The compiled version can be found in the Bootstrap repository (`https://github.com/twbs/bootstrap/releases`).

With regard to using flexbox, you will have limited browser support, since not all browsers are ready for this property. Consider using it if you will have access only from new browsers, such as Internet Explorer versions newer than v10.

Check out the currently available support for the flexbox property here:

```
http://caniuse.com/#feat=flexbox.
```

Summary

In this chapter, we took a big step towards more complex elements and theory. You deserve congratulations for nailing the first example of this book!

First, we presented icons in Bootstrap! It is a very handy tool to place the perfect icon in a perfect way on your page, by customizing the icon size and color. In version 4 of Bootstrap, they dropped native support for Glyphicons, even though you can still use it as a third-party library.

Then we touched the navigations bar of Bootstrap and presented a bunch of options to customize it for our case. We played with some tricks to collapse the menu in the navigation bar, and added more components to it, such as the button dropdown.

Moreover, we again talked about input grouping by showing some more examples of its usage, such as a group of an input and a button.

Finally, we added some theory to the soup, by introducing flexbox and showing that you can use it in conjunction with Bootstrap in the new version 4.

In the next chapters, we will dive into another example. We will start creating a web app! For that, expect the use of even more Bootstrap elements and components. By the end of the explanation, you will be qualified to create any web application!

6

Can You Build a Web App?

Among all kinds of web pages, the web application is the one with the fastest growth in usage. So, we will take a deep dive into this area by developing a really nice web application. Actually, Bootstrap was mainly designed for this type of application, since it was developed at first for the Twitter web application.

Therefore, in this chapter and in the next ones, we will take the reverse path. Instead of developing Bootstrap for Twitter, we will develop an app like Twitter with Bootstrap. With that, we will touch upon even more components and elements of Bootstrap, as follows:

- Web application definitions
- A fully customized navigation bar
- Cards
- Thumbnails
- Pagination
- Breadcrumbs

This chapter will be a bit more difficult, but I believe you are ready for this. So, can you build a web app?

Understanding web applications

Web applications came from the mix of an application and a browser, of course! Basically, a web application is a client application that runs on a web browser. Thus most of the processes are done on the client machine and the server is just responsible for the data processing.

This is interesting, since you can always deliver to the client the most updated version of the application, while the client does not need to upgrade the software. This leads to fast-paced and continuous development of the app.

Creating the code structure

Just as we always say when starting a new example, let's use the HTML boilerplate that we always use, keeping the same folder structure and so on:

```
<!DOCTYPE html>
<html>
  <head>
    <meta charset="utf-8">
    <meta http-equiv="X-UA-Compatible" content="IE=edge">
    <meta name="viewport" content="width=device-width, initial-
scale=1">
    <title>Web App</title>

    <link rel="stylesheet" href="css/bootstrap.css">
    <link rel="stylesheet" href="css/base.css">

    <!--[if lt IE 9]>
      <script
src="https://oss.maxcdn.com/html5shiv/3.7.2/html5shiv.min.js">
</script>
      <script
src="https://oss.maxcdn.com/respond/1.4.2/respond.min.js">
</script>
    <![endif]-->
  </head>
  <body>
    <script src="js/jquery-1.11.3.js"></script>
    <script src="js/bootstrap.js"></script>
    <script src="js/main.js"></script>
  </body>
</html>
```

Adding the navigation

First of all, we will add the navigation bar to our web application. Before the start of the <body> tag, add the navigation bar, just as we did in the last chapter:

```
<nav class="navbar navbar-default navbar-fixed-top">
  <div class="container">
```

```
      <div class="navbar-header">
        <a class="navbar-brand" href="webapp.html">
          <img src="imgs/logo.png" class="img-responsive">
        </a>
        <button type="button" class="navbar-toggle collapsed" data-
    toggle="collapse" data-target="#nav-menu" aria-expanded="false">
          <span class="sr-only">Toggle navigation</span>
          <span class="icon-bar"></span>
          <span class="icon-bar"></span>
          <span class="icon-bar"></span>
        </button>
        <!-- <a class="btn btn-primary navbar-btn pull-left"
    href="#" role="button">Sign up</a> -->
      </div>

      <div id="nav-menu" class="collapse navbar-collapse">
          <ul class="nav navbar-nav">
          </ul>
      </div>
    </div>
</nav>
```

First, we created a simple navigation bar with the collapse option, just as we did in the last chapter. The major difference this time is the addition of the image `<img src="imgs/logo.png" class="img-responsive">` logo. The CSS for adjusting the logo is as follows:

```
.navbar-brand img {
  height: 100%
}
```

So, we need to create the items inside the list `ul.nav.navbar-nav` tag. Append the following code inside the list:

```
<ul class="nav navbar-nav">
  <li>
    <a href="#">
      Home
    </a>
  </li>
  <li>
    <a href="#">
      Notifications
    </a>
  </li>
  <li>
```

```
    <a href="#">
      Messages
    </a>
  </li>
</ul>
```

Therefore, we should add some icons to each menu. Do you remember how to do this? We need to use the Bootstrap Glyphicons. Add the icons, as highlighted in this HTML code:

```
<ul class="nav navbar-nav">
  <li>
    <a href="#">
      <span class="glyphicon glyphicon-home" aria-hidden="true"></
span>
      Home
    </a>
  </li>
  <li>
    <a href="#">
      <span class="glyphicon glyphicon-bell" aria-hidden="true"></
span>
      Notifications
    </a>
  </li>
  <li>
    <a href="#">
      <span class="glyphicon glyphicon-envelope" aria-hidden="true"></
span>
      Messages
    </a>
  </li>
</ul>
```

The result right now should look like what is shown in the following screenshot:

Adding the search input

In our navigation bar, we will add a search input. There are two tricks for this. The first is the input must be like an input group to have a magnifier icon on the right-hand-side part. The second is that the input must be aligned to the right and not to the left in the `<nav>`. In the HTML, let's create a form after `ul.nav.navbar-nav`:

```html
<div id="nav-menu" class="collapse navbar-collapse">
    <ul class="nav navbar-nav">
      ...
    </ul>

    <form id="search" role="search">
      <div class="input-group">
         <input type="text" class="form-control"
placeholder="Search...">
         <span class="glyphicon glyphicon-search" aria-hidden="true"></
span>
      </div>
    </form>
</div>
```

In the CSS, move the form to the right and add some padding:

```css
nav form#search {
  float: right;
  padding: 0.5em;
}

nav form#search .glyphicon-search {
    z-index: 99;
    position: absolute;
    right: 0.7em;
    top: 50%;
    margin-top: -0.44em;
}

nav form#search .input-group .form-control {
    border-radius: 0.25em;
}
```

Refresh the web page and check out the input. It should appear as shown in this screenshot:

Time for the menu options!

Our navigation bar is starting to appear like the navigation bar of a web application, but not close enough! Now, it's the turn of the menu options.

The option at the thumbnail

We will now do some crazy stuff: add a thumbnail together with a Bootstrap button dropdown. Just before `form#search`, add the button HTML:

```
<div id="nav-options" class="btn-group pull-right">
  <button type="button" class="btn btn-default dropdown-toggle
thumbnail" data-toggle="dropdown" aria-haspopup="true" aria-
expanded="false">
    <img src="imgs/jon.png">
  </button>
  <ul class="dropdown-menu">
    <li><a href="#">Profile</a></li>
    <li><a href="#">Setting</a></li>
    <li role="separator" class="divider"></li>
    <li><a href="#">Logout</a></li>
  </ul>
</div>
```

Basically, we used the template for a button dropdown (which you learned about in the previous chapter) and just removed the `.caret` component present on it. Instead of adding some text, we added an image, that is, the profile image. In `.btn-group`, we applied the helper class from Bootstrap, `.pull-right`. Since it was placed before the form, the button will appear after the form.

Then, it's time for the CSS. We need to resize the image and properly set the margins and paddings:

```
#nav-options {
  margin: 0.5em;
}

#nav-options button.thumbnail {
```

```
  margin: 0;
  padding: 0;
}


#nav-options img {
  max-height: 2.3em;
  border-radius: 0.3em;
}
```

The result of the addition of the button should be like what is shown in the following screenshot:

Adding the Tweet button

The last element present in the navigation bar is the **Tweet** button. To add it, we set following the HTML right before the button group option that we just added:

```
<button id="tweet" class="btn btn-default pull-right">
  <span class="glyphicon glyphicon-pencil" aria-hidden="true"></span>
  Tweet
</button>
```

For the CSS, we just need to add some margin:

```
#tweet {
  margin: 0.5em;
}
```

Finally, we have all the elements and components in our navigation bar, and it should look like this:

Customizing the navigation bar

Now that we have our navigation bar done, it's time to customize the Bootstrap theme, add some tweaks, and fix viewport issues.

Setting up the custom theme

To be a little different, we will use a blue background color for our navigation bar. First, we need to add some simple CSS rules:

```
.navbar-default {
  background-color: #2F92CA;
}

.navbar-default .navbar-nav > li > a {
  color: #FFF;
}
```

Afterwards, let's add the active option to the list on the navigation. Add the .active class to the first element of the nav list (the **Home** one), presented in bold in the following code:

```
<ul class="nav navbar-nav">
  <li class="active">
    <a href="#">
    <span class="glyphicon glyphicon-home" aria-hidden="true"></
span>
      Home
    </a>
  </li>
  … <!--others li and the rest of the code -->
</ul>
```

Then, go to the CSS and set the following:

```
.navbar-default {
  background-color: #2F92CA;
}

.navbar-default .navbar-nav > li > a {
  color: #FFF;
}

.navbar-default .navbar-nav > .active > a {
  background-color: transparent;
  color: #FFF;
```

```
        padding-bottom: 10px;
        border-bottom: 5px solid #FFF;
    }
```

The result of this should be like the one presented in the following screenshot. You can see that **Home** is in the active state. To mark that, we've added a border below it for denotation:

Fixing the list navigation bar pseudo-classes

If you hover over any element in the navigation list, you will see that it has the wrong color. We will use some style to fix that—by using CSS3 transitions! The complete CSS for the customization should be like the following:

```css
.navbar-default {
  background-color: #2F92CA;
}

.navbar-default .navbar-nav > li > a,
.navbar-default .navbar-nav > li > a:hover {
  color: #FFF;
  -webkit-transition: all 150ms ease-in-out;
  -moz-transition: all 150ms ease-in-out;
  -ms-transition: all 150ms ease-in-out;
  -o-transition: all 150ms ease-in-out;
  transition: all 150ms ease-in-out;
}

.navbar-default .navbar-nav > .active > a {
  background-color: transparent;
  color: #FFF;
  padding-bottom: 0.62em;
  border-bottom: 0.45em solid #FFF;}

.navbar-default .navbar-nav > .active > a:hover,
.navbar-default .navbar-nav > li > a:hover {
  background-color: transparent;
  color: #F3F3F3;
  padding-bottom: 0.62em;
  border-bottom: 0.45em solid #F3F3F3;
}
```

CSS3 transitions

Transitions are an addition of CSS3 that allow us to change a property smoothly. We can pass in order the property (in our case, we used `all`), the time to complete the transition, and the animation function (we used `ease-in-out`).

Here, we had to change the default colors from the default Bootstrap navigation list. Also, by adding the transitions, we got a nice effect; when the user hovers over the menu, a border appears at the bottom of the item list.

You deserve a badge!

To finish the navigation bar, it would be nice to add some badges to the notifications item in the up list to show the number of new notifications, just as Twitter has on its website. For that, you will learn to use Bootstrap badges.

So, in the notifications item in the list, add the following highlighted HTML line:

```
<ul class="nav navbar-nav">
  <li class="active">
    <a href="#">
      <span class="glyphicon glyphicon-home" aria-hidden="true"></
span>
      Home
    </a>
  </li>
  <li>
    <a href="#">
      <span class="badge">5</span>
      <span class="glyphicon glyphicon-bell" aria-hidden="true"></
span>
      Notifications
    </a>
  </li>
  <li>
    <a href="#">
      <span class="glyphicon glyphicon-envelope" aria-hidden="true"></
span>
      Messages
    </a>
  </li>
</ul>
```

For the CSS, set some positions, paddings, and borders:

```
.navbar-nav .badge {
  color: #2F92CA;
  background-color: #FFF;
  font-size: 0.7em;
  padding: 0.27rem 0.55rem 0.2rem 0.4rem;
  position: absolute;
  left: 0.37rem;
  top: 0.7rem;
  z-index: 99;
  border: 0.2rem solid #2F92CA;
}
```

Nicely done! Refresh the browser and you will see this pretty, beautiful badge:

Fixing some issues with the navigation bar

We now have three issues with the navigation bar. Can you guess them?

They are the **Tweet** button at the small viewport, the collapsed navigation menu collapse, and the color of the collapse *hamburger* button.

Well, first we will handle the easiest one—fix the **Tweet** button! For that, we will create another element to be placed at the left-hand side of the collapse button and just display it when they are in extra small resolution. First, add the `.hidden-xs` class to the current `Tweet` button:

```
<button id="tweet" class="btn btn-default pull-right hidden-xs">
  <span class="glyphicon glyphicon-pencil" aria-hidden="true"></span>
  Tweet
</button>
```

Secondly, at `.navbar-header`, after `button.navbar-toggle`, add the following highlighted button:

```
<div class="navbar-header">
  <a class="navbar-brand" href="webapp.html">
    <img src="imgs/logo.png" class="img-responsive">
  </a>
```

```
<button type="button" class="navbar-toggle collapsed" data-
toggle="collapse" data-target="#nav-menu" aria-expanded="false">
    <span class="sr-only">Toggle navigation</span>
    <span class="icon-bar"></span>
    <span class="icon-bar"></span>
    <span class="icon-bar"></span>
</button>

<button id="tweet" class="btn btn-default pull-right visible-xs-
block">
    <span class="glyphicon glyphicon-pencil" aria-hidden="true"></
span>
    Tweet
</button>
</div>
```

So, what we did is hide the **Tweet** button for extra small devices and show a new one in a different element. Set a mobile viewport and you can see the button's position fixed, as follows:

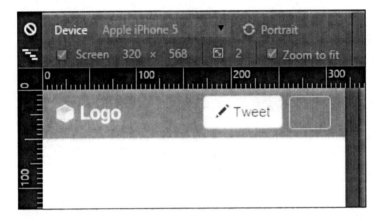

Next, let's fix the color of the collapse *hamburger* button. Just apply the next CSS to change its color:

```
.navbar-header .navbar-toggle,
.navbar-default .navbar-toggle:focus {
  background-color: #57A5D2;
}

.navbar-default .navbar-toggle:hover {
  background-color: #3986B3;
}
```

```
.navbar-default .navbar-toggle .icon-bar {
  background-color: #FFF;
}
```

Finally, let's customize the collapsed navigation bar using Bootstrap helpers. We add the `.hidden-xs` class to `.nav-options` and the `.hidden-sm` class to the `form#search` element, making them invisible for extra small and small devices respectively, just as we did to the **Tweet** button:

```
<div id="nav-options" class="btn-group pull-right hidden-xs">
  ...
</div>

<form id="search" role="search" class="hidden-sm">
  ...
</form>
```

Then, in the `ul.nav.navbar-nav` navigation list, create two items that will replace the ones hidden at the current viewport:

```
<ul class="nav navbar-nav">
  . . .
  <!-- others elements list were hidden -->
  <li class="visible-xs-inline">
    <a href="#">
      <span class="glyphicon glyphicon-user" aria-hidden="true"></
span>
      Profile
    </a>
  </li>
  <li class="visible-xs-inline">
    <a href="#">
      <span class="glyphicon glyphicon-off" aria-hidden="true"></span>
      Logout
    </a>
  </li>
</ul>
```

Thus we are making them visible for extra small resolution with the `.visible.xs-inline` class, as long they are from an inline list.

To wrap it up, let's remove the border in the active list item, since it does not seem nice at the bottom in the layout. Let's change it to a right border instead of bottom with the following CSS using a media query:

```
@media (max-width:34em){
  .navbar-default .navbar-nav > .active > a {
    border-bottom: none;
    border-left: 0.45em solid #FFF;
    padding-left: 0.5em;
  }
}
```

And we are done! Refresh the web page and see the final result of the navigation bar. It is awesome!

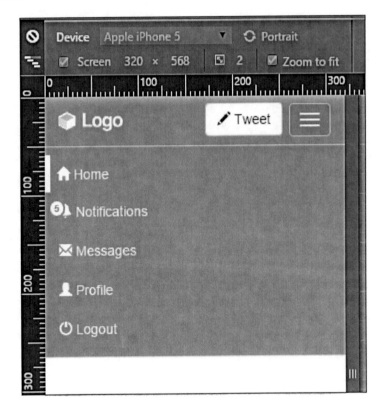

Do a grid again

We have finally finished the navigation bar. Now it's time to the page main content. For that, we must create a page grid. Following how Twitter uses a three-column-based layout, we will do the same. The HTML code for the scaffolding is the one that should be placed after the `<nav>` element:

```
<div class="container">
  <div class="row">
    <div id="profile" class="col-md-3 hidden-sm hidden-xs"></div>
    <div id="main" class="col-sm-12 col-md-6"> </div>
    <div id="right-content" class="col-md-3 hidden-sm hidden-xs"> </
div>
  </div>
</div>
```

To understand it, we just created a `.container` with a single `.row`. The `.row` contains three columns, the first and the last being visible only for medium and larger devices. This is because of the `.hidden-sm` and `.hidden-xs` classes. When both columns are hidden, the middle column fills the row completely. This is because of the `.col-sm-12` class.

To finish that, add a `padding-top` to `<body>` in order to correct the page's position with respect to the navigation bar:

```
body {
  padding-top: 4em;
  background-color: #F5F8FA;
}
```

Playing the cards

Moving on, in our web application, we will create a new component containing the about information, named *Card*. We will take a break from page development to discuss this section in depth.

Cards are flexible container extensions that include internal options, such as header, footer, and other display options. In Bootstrap 4, there is a component called Card, but since we are supporting versions 3 and 4 in this book, we will teach both ways.

Learning cards in Bootstrap 4

As was mentioned before, Bootstrap 4 provides Cards components. To make use of them, create a `div.card` element and start adding elements such as `.card-block` and `.card-img-top`:

```
<div class="card">
  <img class="card-img-top img-responsive"
src="imgs/landscape.jpg">
  <div class="card-block">
    <h4 class="card-title">Name</h4>
    <p class="card-text">About text</p>
    <a href="#" class="btn btn-primary">Can add buttons</a>
  </div>
</div>
```

For the preceding code, the output will look like what is shown in the following screenshot. As we can see, the Card component is pretty simple and straightforward. The component offers some other options as well, but we will talk about that when needed.

Creating your own cards

Like the famous quote, *if you have lemons, make lemonade*, in Bootstrap version 3, we do not have the Card component. However, we have the tools needed to make our own Card component for sure! So let's have some lemonade!

We will use the same classes and structures of Bootstrap 4, playing with only the CSS. Therefore, if you are using version 3, you will see the page render like this for the use of the same HTML from version 4:

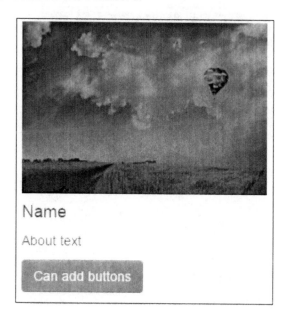

To squeeze the first lemon, let's create the CSS for the .card class:

```
.card {
  position: relative;
  border: 0.1rem solid #e5e5e5;
  border-radius: 0.4rem;
  position: relative;
  background-color: #FFF;
}
```

Following this, just add two CSS rules for img.card-img-top and .card-block, as shown here:

```
.card-img-top {
  border-radius: 0.4rem 0.4rem 0 0;
}
```

```
.card-block {
  padding: 1.25rem;
}
```

Done! We have our own card component ready for Bootstrap 3. The next screenshot presents the final result. Of course, there are some differences of typography and button color, but these are the differences because of the version; the component is perfectly done.

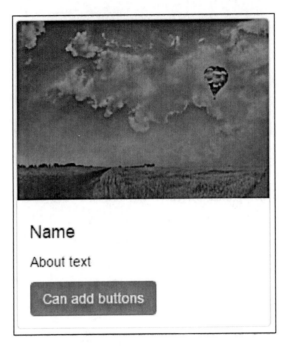

Can you finish the Card component?

We presented just a few options for the Card component in Bootstrap version 3. Can you do the rest? Try making some CSS rules for classes such as `.card-img-bottom`, `.card-header`, and `.card-footer`.

Adding Cards to our web application

Getting back to the web application, let's add the Card components inside `div#profile`, at the main container. The HTML code for this section will be as follows:

```
<div id="profile-resume" class="card">
  <img class="card-img-top img-responsive"
src="imgs/landscape.jpg">
```

```html
<div class="card-block">
  <img src="imgs/jon.png" class="card-img">
  <h4 class="card-title">Jonny Doo <small>@jonnydoo</small></h4>
  <p class="card-text">Dog goes woofy. Did you said squitly?</p>
  <ul class="list-inline list-unstyled">
    <li id="card-tweets">
      <a href="#">
        <span class="profile-stats">Tweets</span>
        <span class="profile-value">99k</span>
      </a>
    </li>
    <li class="card-following">
      <a href="#">
        <span class="profile-stats">Following</span>
        <span class="profile-value">7</span>
      </a>
    </li>
    <li class="card-followers">
      <a href="#">
        <span class="profile-stats">Followers</span>
        <span class="profile-value">132k</span>
      </a>
    </li>
  </ul>
</div>
</div>
```

Breaking down the code, we added some components to `.card-block`. First of all is the `.card-img` element, which will represent the profile photography. Following this, we changed `.card-title` by adding a `<small>` tag inside `<h4>`. The last change is the addition of the `<ul>` list, representing some stats for the profile.

There is no secret in this HTML piece; we just added some elements in a straightforward way. Now it's time for the CSS rules. First, change the position and size of the `img.card-img` element:

```css
.card-block img.card-img {
  top: 50%;
  margin-top: -36px;
  width: 72px;
  border: 3px solid #FFF;
  border-radius: 0.4rem;
  float: left;
  position: relative;
  z-index: 99;
}
```

Since it is in the right place, let's correctly align `.card-title` and add some padding to `.card-text`:

```css
.card-block .card-title {
  float: left;
  margin: 0;
  margin-left: 0.5em;
}

.card-block .card-title small {
  display: block;
}

.card-block .card-text {
  clear: both;
  padding-top: 0.25em;
  margin-bottom: 1.5em;
}
```

> **Can you change the card block to use flexbox?**
>
> Another challenge appears here. Since you have already learned about the usage of flexbox, try to replace the floats in the previous code with some flexbox CSS rules. Just keep in mind that it is recommended for Bootstrap 4 and works only on new browsers.

It is almost looking like the Twitter card on the left; we just need to change the list style inside the profile card. Add this CSS:

```css
.card-block ul a:hover {
  text-decoration: none;
}

.card-block ul .profile-stats {
  color: #777;
  display: block;
  text-transform: uppercase;
  font-size: 0.63em;
}

.card-block ul .profile-value {
  color: #000;
  font-size: 1.2em;
  font-weight: bold;
  color: #2F92CA;
}
```

Well done! It looks prettier than the Twitter component. In the following screenshot, we present the expected result:

Another card using thumbnails

After the `#profile-resume` card, we will create another one named `#profile-photo`, which will contain photos of the user. Use the same cards methodology to place this new one after `#profile-resume` with the following HTML code:

```html
<div id="profile-photo" class="card">
  <div class="card-header">Photos</div>
  <div class="card-block">
    <ul class="list-inline list-unstyled">
      <li>
        <a href="#" class="thumbnail"><img class="img-responsive"
src="imgs/landscape-02.jpg"></a>
      </li>
      <li>
        <a href="#" class="thumbnail"><img class="img-responsive"
src="imgs/landscape-03.jpg"></a>
      </li>
      <li>
        <a href="#" class="thumbnail"><img class="img-responsive"
src="imgs/landscape-04.jpg"></a>
      </li>
      <li>
        <a href="#" class="thumbnail"><img class="img-responsive"
src="imgs/landscape-05.jpg"></a>
      </li>
    </ul>
  </div>
</div>
```

In this card we will create a new card element, `.card-header`. In Bootstrap 4, you can use the regarding class, but in version 3, you will need this CSS rule:

```css
.card .card-header {
  border-radius: 0.4rem 0.4rem 0 0;
  padding: .75rem 1.25rem;
  background-color: #f5f5f5;
  border-bottom: 0.1em solid #e5e5e5;
  color: #4e5665;
  font-weight: bold;
}
```

Moving on, the rest of CSS for this card is simple. Just change the image's width and adjust some margins and paddings:

```css
#profile-photo {
  margin-top: 2rem;
}

#profile-photo ul {
  margin: 0;
}

#profile-photo li {
  width: 48%;
  padding: 0;
}
```

Also note that we are using the `.thumbnail` class in the `<a>` tag that wraps the images. This class is useful for nicely styled thumbnail images. It can also be used to wrap text along with an image.

The photo card should look like what is shown in the following screenshot. Again, we will use some more cards in this web application, although we'll talk about that later, when needed.

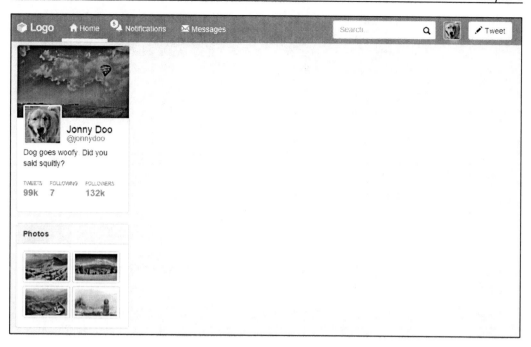

Implementing the main content

Moving on, we will implement the main content in the middle of the page. This content will hold the feeds while allowing new tweets.

We need to create the input to send a new message. To do this, create the following HTML code at the `div#main` element:

```
<div id="main" class="col-sm-12 col-md-6">
  <div id="main-card" class="card">
    <form id="new-message">
      <div class="input-group">
        <input type="text" class="form-control" placeholder="What
is happening?">
        <span class="input-group-addon">
          <span class="glyphicon glyphicon-camera" aria-
hidden="true"></span>
        </span>
      </div>
    </form>
  </div>
</div>
```

For that, we created a form, again making use of input groups, icons, and cards. Can you see the ease provided by Bootstrap again? We just placed the elements with the right classes and everything went perfect. The next CSS takes place with some rules regarding the color and padding of the form:

```
form#new-message {
  border-radius: 0.4rem 0.4rem 0 0;
  padding: 1em;
  border-bottom: 0.1em solid #CEE4F5;
  background-color: #EBF4FB;
}

form#new-message .input-group-addon {
  background-color: #FFF;
}
```

At this point, the result should be as shown in the following screenshot. Next up, we will create the other elements.

Making your feed

We have made cool things so far, but the feed is the core of the page. We will create a nice and friendly feed for our web app.

As usual, let's create the HTML code first. The feed will work inside a stacked list. With that in mind, let's create the first element in the list:

```html
<div id="main" class="col-sm-12 col-md-6">
  <div id="main-card" class="card">
    <form id="new-message">
      <div class="input-group">
        <input type="text" class="form-control" placeholder="What is happening?">
        <span class="input-group-addon">
          <span class="glyphicon glyphicon-camera" aria-hidden="true"></span>
        </span>
      </div>
    </form>
    <ul id="feed" class="list-unstyled">
      <li>
        <img src="imgs/doge.jpg" class="feed-avatar img-circle">
        <div class="feed-post">
          <h5>Name <small>@namex - 3h</small></h5>
          <p> You can't hold a dog down without staying down with him!</p>
        </div>
        <div class="action-list">
          <a href="#">
            <span class="glyphicon glyphicon-share-alt" aria-hidden="true"></span>
          </a>
          <a href="#">
            <span class="glyphicon glyphicon-refresh " aria-hidden="true"></span>
            <span class="retweet-count">6</span>
          </a>
          <a href="#">
            <span class="glyphicon glyphicon-star" aria-hidden="true"></span>
          </a>
        </div>
      </li>
    </ul>
  </div>
</div>
```

The highlighted code is the code added for the list. To understand it, we created an element in the list containing the common stuff inside a post, such as an image, a name, text, and options. Add the `.img-circle` class to the image in the list to style it using Bootstrap image styles.

With the CSS, we will correctly style the page. For the list and the image, apply the following rules:

```
ul#feed {
    margin: 0;
}

ul#feed li {
    padding: 1em 1em;
}

ul#feed .feed-avatar {
    width: 13%;
    display: inline-block;
    vertical-align: top;
}
```

By doing this, you will be correcting the margins and padding while adjusting the size of the image avatar. For the post section, use this CSS:

```
ul#feed .feed-post {
    width: 80%;
    display: inline-block;
    margin-left: 2%;
}

ul#feed .feed-post h5 {
    font-weight: bold;
    margin-bottom: 0.5rem;
}

ul#feed .feed-post h5 > small {
    font-size: 1.2rem;
}
```

Finally, with regard to `.action-list`, set the following styles:

```
ul#feed .action-list {
    margin-left: 13%;
    padding-left: 1em;
}
```

```
ul#feed .action-list a {
  width: 15%;
  display: inline-block;
}

ul#feed .action-list a:hover {
  text-decoration: none;
}

ul#feed .action-list .retweet-count {
  padding-left: 0.2em;
  font-weight: bold;
}
```

Refresh your browser and you will get this result:

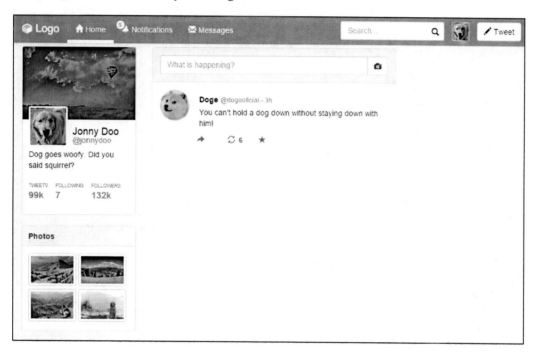

Awesome! Note that for the post, we did all the spacing using percentage values. This is also a great option because the page will resize with respect to the user's resolution very smoothly.

We have only one problem now. Add another post and you will see that there is no divisor between the posts. To illustrate this, add a second post in the HTML code:

```
<ul id="feed" class="list-unstyled">
  <li>
    <img src="imgs/doge.jpg" class="feed-avatar img-circle">
    <div class="feed-post">
      <h5>Doge <small>@dogeoficial - 3h</small></h5>
      <p>You can't hold a dog down without staying down with
him!</p>
    </div>
    <div class="action-list">
      <a href="#">
        <span class="glyphicon glyphicon-share-alt" aria-
hidden="true"></span>
      </a>
      <a href="#">
        <span class="glyphicon glyphicon-refresh" aria-
hidden="true"></span>
        <span class="retweet-count">6</span>
      </a>
      <a href="#">
        <span class="glyphicon glyphicon-star" aria-hidden="true"></
span>
      </a>
    </div>
  </li>

  <li>
    <img src="imgs/laika.jpg" class="feed-avatar img-circle">
    <div class="feed-post">
      <h5>Laika <small>@spacesog - 4h</small></h5>
      <p>That's one small step for a dog, one giant leap for
giant</p>
    </div>
    <div class="action-list">
      <a href="#">
        <span class="glyphicon glyphicon-share-alt" aria-
hidden="true"></span>
      </a>
      <a href="#">
        <span class="glyphicon glyphicon-refresh" aria-
hidden="true"></span>
        <span class="retweet-count">6</span>
      </a>
```

```
      <a href="#">
        <span class="glyphicon glyphicon-star" aria-hidden="true"></
span>
      </a>
    </div>
  </li>
</ul>
```

At the CSS, change it a little to correct the padding and add a border between the items, as follows:

```
ul#feed li {
  padding: 1em 1em;
  border-bottom: 0.1rem solid #e5e5e5;
}

ul#feed li:last-child {
  border-bottom: none;
}
```

The output results will be like this:

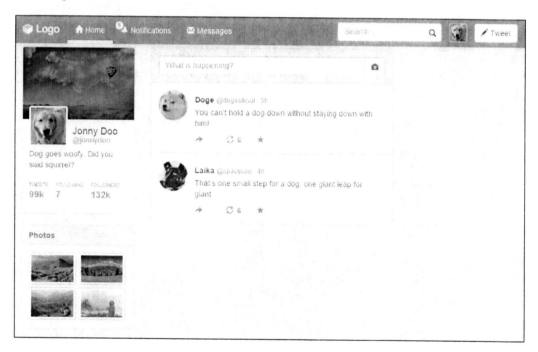

Doing some pagination

Okay, I know that web applications such as Twitter usually use infinite loading and not pagination, but we need to learn that! Bootstrap offers incredible options for pagination, so let's use some of them right now.

From the start, create the HTML code for the component and insert it just after `div`. `main-card`:

```
<nav class="text-center">
  <ul class="pagination pagination-lg">
    <li class="disabled"><a href="#" aria-label="Previous"><span
aria-hidden="true">&laquo;</span></a></li>
    <li class="active"><a href="#">1 <span class="sr-only">(current)</
span></a></li>
    <li><a href="#">2</a></li>
    <li class="disabled"><a href="#">...</a></li>
    <li><a href="#">3</a></li>
    <li><a href="#">4</a></li>
    <li><a href="#" aria-label="Next"><span aria-
hidden="true">&raquo;</span></a></li>
  </ul>
</nav>
```

Thus, we must consider a few things here. Firstly, to center the pagination, we used the helper class from Bootstrap, `.text-center`. This is because `ul.pagination` does apply the `display: inline-block` style.

Secondly, we created a `<ul>` with the `.pagination` class, determined by the framework. We also added the `.pagination-lg` class, which is an option of pagination for making it bigger.

Lastly, the `.disabled` class is present in two items of the list, the previous link and the ellipsis . . . one. Also, the list on page 1 is marked as active, changing its background color.

Check out the result of adding pagination in this screenshot:

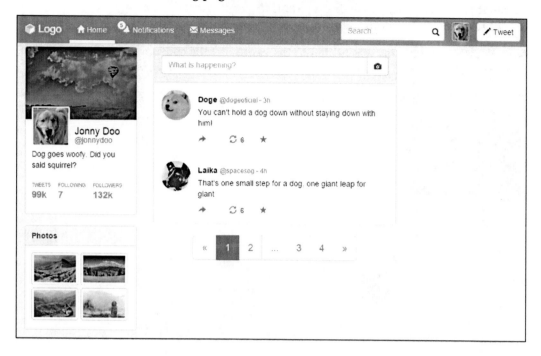

Creating breadcrumbs

To make use of Bootstrap breadcrumbs, we will add it to our web app. Note that we will do this step for learning purposes so that you will be able to create it when you need it.

Like pagination, Bootstrap offers a component for breadcrumbs as well. For that, create an ordered list just after the open tag div#main:

```
<div id="main" class="col-sm-12 col-md-6">

  <ol class="breadcrumb card">
    <li><a href="#">Home</a></li>
    <li><a href="#">Profile</a></li>
    <li class="active">Feed</li>
  </ol>
  ...
</div>
```

The cool thing about Bootstrap breadcrumbs is that the separator bars are automatically added through :before and the content CSS option, so you do not need to worry about them.

Note that the .card class was added to the breadcrumbs component to keep the web app style. The following screenshot presents the result of breadcrumbs:

Finishing with the right-hand-side content

Well, we are almost done. It is time to create the right-hand-side content of our web app. The right-hand-side content contains information such as *Whom to follow* and the about page. Let's create it!

Coming to the HTML, let's create another Card component inside div.right-content, as follows:

```
<div id="right-content" class="col-md-3 hidden-sm hidden-xs">
  <div id="who-follow" class="card">
    <div class="card-header">
      Who to follow
    </div>
```

```
    <div class="card-block">

    </div>
  </div>
</div>
```

Inside `.card-block`, create a vertical list:

```
<div id="right-content" class="col-md-3 hidden-sm hidden-xs">
  <div id="who-follow" class="card">
    <div class="card-header">
      Who to follow
    </div>
    <div class="card-block">
      <ul class="list-unstyled">
        <li>
          <img src="imgs/cat.jpg" class="img-rounded">
          <div class="info">
            <strong>Crazy cats</strong>
            <button class="btn btn-default">
              <span class="glyphicon glyphicon-plus" aria-
hidden="true"></span> Follow
            </button>
          </div>
        </li>
        <li>
          <img src="imgs/ration.jpg" class="img-rounded">
          <div class="info">
            <strong>Free ration alert</strong>
            <button class="btn btn-default">
              <span class="glyphicon glyphicon-plus" aria-
hidden="true"></span> Follow
            </button>
          </div>
        </li>
      </ul>
    </div>
  </div>
</div>
```

So, the result without the CSS is not good, as shown in the following screenshot. We need to fix it.

First, we add margins for the items in the list:

```
div#who-follow li {
  margin-bottom: 2em;
}

div#who-follow li:last-child {
  margin-bottom: 0;
}
```

Then, we adjust the size of the image and the following text:

```
div#who-follow li img {
  width: 26%;
  display: inline-block;
  vertical-align: top;
```

```
    margin-right: 2%;
}

div#who-follow li .info {
  width: 68%;
  display: inline-block;
}
```

To finish this, we adjust the content inside the `.info` element:

```
div#who-follow li .info strong {
  display: block;
  overflow:hidden;
  text-overflow: ellipsis;
}

div#who-follow li .info .glyphicon {
  color: #2F92CA;
}
```

The result should look like what is shown here:

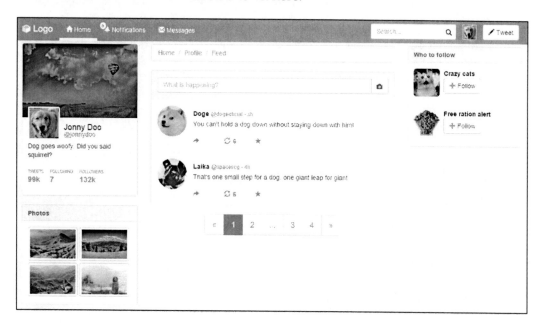

To end the main web page content, let's create another card that has content about the web page, such as help, privacy, and so on. After the `div#who-follow`, create another card:

```html
<div id="app-info" class="card">
  <div class="card-block">
    © 2015 SampleApp
    <ul class="list-unstyled list-inline">
      <li><a href="#">About</a></li>
      <li><a href="#">Terms and Privacy</a></li>
      <li><a href="#">Help</a></li>
      <li><a href="#">Status</a></li>
      <li><a href="#">Contact</a></li>
    </ul>
  </div>
  <div class="card-footer">
    <a href="#">Connect other address book</a>
  </div>
</div>
```

First of all, note that we have just used `.card-footer` for this card. If you are using Bootstrap 3, add the next CSS:

```css
.card .card-footer {
  border-radius: 0 0 0.4rem 0.4rem;
  padding: .75rem 1.25rem;
  background-color: #f5f5f5;
  border-top: 0.1em solid #e5e5e5;
  color: #4e5665;
}
```

For this card, we also need to add some margin within the card above:

```css
div#app-info {
  margin-top: 2rem;
}
```

That looks great! We have finished the majority of the components in our web application! The next image shows the final result that we will cover at this chapter. Great work!

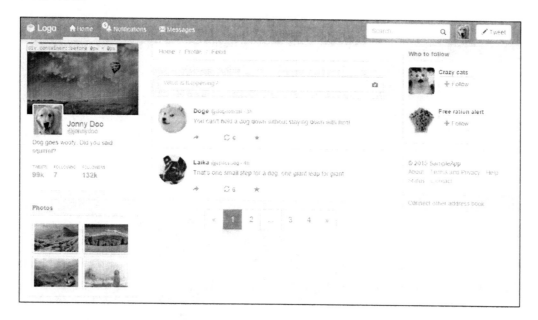

Summary

In this chapter, we started the development of another example—an awesome web application like Twitter. We started creating every component with the help of Bootstrap, while also customizing each one. By the end of the chapter, we were done with the major part of the components to be added.

First, we created a fully customized navigation bar that works on any device. Just like at every component, we took special care with different visualizations for mobiles and desktops.

We talked a lot about cards. This is a new component in Bootstrap 4, but we created our own for version 3, so we nailed it all. Cards are present in every column, having different content and placements of items.

We also discussed the use of other Bootstrap components by making use of breadcrumbs, pagination, and thumbnails.

I hope now you feel confident about web application development, because in the next chapter, we will take a step further in this kind of development by using other Bootstrap components and more customization.

7
Of Course, You Can Build a Web App!

In this chapter, we will complete the elements of our web app with the use of other Bootstrap elements and components. By the end of this chapter, we will have covered the majority of elements present in Bootstrap, making you almost an expert as well as answering this question from the last chapter: can you build a web app? Of course you can!

We will cover some more complex Bootstrap components and elements. These are the key points of this chapter, and you will learn how to:

- Use Bootstrap alerts
- Customize alerts
- Progress bars
- CSS key frames
- Navigation components
- Tabs
- Labels and badges
- List groups

Even though these seem to be a lot of key points, they are easy to learn and master. So, I am sure you will be able to nail all of them.

Alerts in our web app

In the last chapter, we did almost everything related to page components. Now we will create some components that interact with the user. To start this, we will introduce alerts, which are very common components of every web app.

In order to learn about alerts, we should create some of them. The pattern for creation is pretty simple; just remember to import Bootstrap JavaScript as we have been doing all throughout the book.

The main class needed to create alerts is `.alert`. You can just follow this class with some other, regarding the type of alert, such as `.alert-success` for a success message. There are other classes available as well, such as `.alert-info` and `.alert-danger`. Just replace the suffix of `.alert` with the one that you want to use.

It's time to create our first alert! Keeping the same code of the web app from the last chapter, right before `div#main`, you must have your `ol.breadcrumb`. Replace `ol.breadcrumb` with your `.alert`, like what is shown in this screenshot:

The HTML code for creating this alert is really simple:

```
<div class="alert alert-success" role="alert">
  You have made a new Tweet.
</div>
```

As mentioned before, just create an element with the `.alert` class in combination with the state of the alert, `.alert-success` in this case.

> **Why do we use the role attribute?**
>
> In the preceding example, we made use of the `role="alert"` attribute in our `.alert` component. The role attribute was incorporated into HTML 5, coming from the ARIA 1.0 specification. The reason for using that is to keep the semantics for different items, for example, in this case, where we used a common `<div>` to describe a more semantic element that is an alert.

Dismissing alerts

Bootstrap is incredible! Did you realize that? We created an alert with just three lines of code!

Well, another reason to think about that is to create dismissible alerts. Just add the highlighted line to the alert component and you will get the expected result:

```
<div class="alert alert-success" role="alert">
  <button type="button" class="close" data-dismiss="alert" aria-
label="Close"><span aria-hidden="true">&times;</span></button>
  You have made a new Tweet.
</div>
```

This will create a close button that will dismiss the component using the `data-dismiss="alert"` attribute. Refresh the web page and you will see the alert like this:

You have made a new Tweet.   x

Customizing alerts

Now, it's time for us to create our recipe for the alert. We have two tasks: add a title to `.alert` and use the links inside it.

First, create a heading element inside the alert:

```
<div class="alert alert-success" role="alert">
  <button type="button" class="close" data-dismiss="alert" aria-
label="Close"><span aria-hidden="true">&times;</span></button>
  <h3>Tweet alert</h3>
  You have made a new Tweet.
</div>
```

Then, adjust the CSS for the heading inside the alert:

```
.alert h3 {
  margin: 0   0 1rem;
  font-size: 1.4em;
}
```

The final result of adding the title must be like what is shown in this screenshot:

For the second task, we have to add some links inside the component. Bootstrap can give us a little shortcut for this using the .alert-link class in the link. The class will give the correctly matching color for the link in response to the kind of the alert shown.

Therefore, the HTML code is simple:

```
<div class="alert alert-success" role="alert">
  <button type="button" class="close" data-dismiss="alert" aria-
label="Close"><span aria-hidden="true">&times;</span></button>
  <h3>Tweet alert</h3>
  You have made a new Tweet.
  <a href="#" class="alert-link">Click here to review your
tweets.</a>
</div>
```

To finish our first alert usage, let's just add one last fancy thing in the CSS, refresh the browser after that, and check the final result, as shown in the next screenshot:

```
.alert {
  border-left-width: 0.5rem;
}
```

Waiting for the progress bar

Progress bars are very useful in web applications in cases where, for example, you need to wait for an action to be sent to the server while maintaining a feedback for the user that something is being done in the background.

For instance, we can create a progress bar to present the user that a new tweet is being posted. Likewise, other scenarios can suit well for a progress bar, for example, when you are uploading a file on the server or when the web client is loading some information.

To exemplify this, we will create another alert that will contain a progress bar inside for a new tweet post feedback, subliminally saying "Hey, wait until I finish my task!"

We replace the .alert code that we just created with the new one presented here:

```
<div class="alert alert-info" role="alert">
  <button type="button" class="close" data-dismiss="alert" aria-
label="Close"><span aria-hidden="true">&times;</span></button>
  <h3>Posting new Tweet</h3>
</div>
```

This will produce a blue alert using the colors from .alert-info. In the new element, create the following code for the progress bar:

```
<div class="alert alert-info" role="alert">
  <button type="button" class="close" data-dismiss="alert" aria-
label="Close"><span aria-hidden="true">&times;</span></button>
  <h3>Posting new Tweet</h3>
  <div class="progress">
    <div class="progress-bar progress-bar-info" role="progressbar"
aria-valuenow="25" aria-valuemin="0" aria-valuemax="100"
style="width: 25%">
    </div>
  </div>
</div>
```

The result of the progress bar in shown in the next screenshot. Let's understand each part of the new component:

We created a `div.progress` inside our alert component, which is the gray rectangle to be filled during the progress. Inside it, we have another tag, `div.progress-bar`, to create the inside filler that contains the `.progress-bar-info` class to make the bar blue, following the `.info` contextual color.

The progress bar also has some `aria-*` attributes and its size is set by the `width: 25%` style. To change its size, just change the width style.

Progress bar options

Just like alerts, progress bars have the same contextual colors of Bootstrap. Just use the `.progress-bar-*` prefix while using the suffix of one of the contextual colors. It is also possible to apply stripe marks to the progress bar with the `.progress-bar-striped` class:

```
<div class="alert alert-info" role="alert">
  <button type="button" class="close" data-dismiss="alert" aria-label="Close"><span aria-hidden="true">&times;</span></button>
  <h3>Posting new Tweet</h3>
  <div class="progress">
```

```
    <div class="progress-bar progress-bar-info progress-bar-striped
active" role="progressbar" aria-valuenow="25" aria-valuemin="0"
aria-valuemax="100" style="width: 25%">
    </div>
  </div>
</div>
```

Finally, you can also animate the strip using the `.active` class in conjunction with the `.progress-bar-striped` class. Check out the next screenshot to see the result of addition of the classes:

Animating the progress bar

Now we have a good opportunity to use the CSS `@keyframes` animations.

If you check out the CSS code when you add the `.progress-bar-striped` and `.active` classes, Bootstrap will load the following animation:

```
.progress-bar.active {
    animation: progress-bar-stripes 2s linear infinite;
}
```

This animation applies to the CSS selector, the `@keyframe` defined at `progress-bar-stripes`:

```
@keyframes progress-bar-stripes {
  from {
    background-position: 40px 0;
  }
  to {
    background-position: 0 0;
  }
}
```

This means that the striped background will move from a position of 40 pixels to 0, repeating it every 2 seconds.

Well, nice to meet you `progress-bar-stripes`, but I can do another animation! Create the following `@keyframe`:

```
@keyframes w70 {
  from { width: 0%; }
  to { width: 70%; }
}
```

The goal of this key frame is to change the width of our progress bar from 0% to 70% of the maximum when the page loads. Now apply the new animation to `.progress-bar.active`:

```
.progress-bar.active {
  animation: w70 1s ease forwards,
             progress-bar-stripes 2s linear infinite;
}
```

So, our animation will last 1 second and execute just once, since we defined it to be just `forwards`. Note that we must override the animations, so after the new animation, which is `w70`, add the current animation, which is `progress-bar-stripes`. Refresh the page and see this fancy effect.

Creating a settings page

Moving on with our web app example, it is time to create a settings page for the application. We have already created a link for this in the navigation bar, inside the button group. Do you remember?

So, in the same folder as that of the web app HTML file, create another one named `settings.html` and update the link at the navigation bar:

```
<div id="nav-options" class="btn-group pull-right hidden-xs">
  <button type="button" class="btn btn-default dropdown-toggle
thumbnail" data-toggle="dropdown" aria-haspopup="true" aria-
expanded="false">
    <img src="imgs/jon.png">
  </button>
  <ul class="dropdown-menu">
    <li><a href="#">Profile</a></li>
    <li><a href="settings.html">Setting</a></li>
    <li role="separator" class="divider"></li>
    <li><a href="#">Logout</a></li>
  </ul>
</div>
```

In this page, we use the same template that we used in the web application, copying the navigation bar, the grid layout, and the left-hand side #profile column. So, the settings page will look like this:

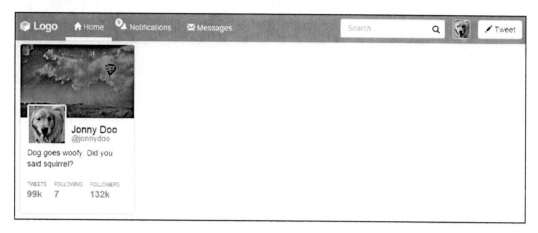

Now we will add some content to this page. Our main goal here is to use some other navigation Bootstrap components that will be handy for us.

Pills of stack

The first navigation menu that we will use here is Pills, using the vertical stack option. Pills are a Bootstrap component used to create menus that can be horizontal or vertical. Many web apps use them for side menus, just as we will soon do.

The basic usage for navigation components is the use of the .nav class followed by another one regarding the navigation option. In our case, we will use the .nav-pills class to create the desired effect in conjunction with the .nav-stacked class to vertically stack the pills. Create a .card element just after #profile and add the code related to the pills navigation:

```
<div id="profile-settings" class="card">
  <ul class="nav nav-pills nav-stacked">
    <li role="presentation" class="active">
      <a href="#">
        Account
        <span class="glyphicon glyphicon-chevron-right pull-right"
aria-hidden="true"></span>
      </a>
    </li>
```

```
      <li role="presentation">
        <a href="#">
          Security
          <span class="glyphicon glyphicon-chevron-right pull-right"
aria-hidden="true"></span>
        </a>
      </li>
      <li role="presentation">
        <a href="#">
          Notifications
          <span class="glyphicon glyphicon-chevron-right pull-right"
aria-hidden="true"></span>
        </a>
      </li>
      <li role="presentation">
        <a href="#">
          Design
          <span class="glyphicon glyphicon-chevron-right pull-right"
aria-hidden="true"></span>
        </a>
      </li>
    </ul>
</div>
```

In the CSS file, also add the following rule:

```
.row .card + .card {
  margin-top: 2rem;
}
```

With this, every .card element followed by another .card element will automatically create a margin, because of the use of the + selector. Open the settings page, and you will see the result like what is shown in the following screenshot:

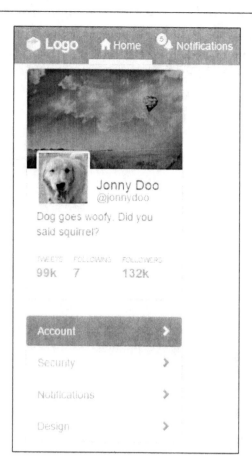

Basically, we created a list with the mentioned classes: `.nav`, `.nav-pills`, and `.nav-stacked`. The list is composed of four items, containing a link and a left arrow icon. To place the arrows at the right-hand side, we again used the `.pull-right` helper together with the `.glyphicon-chevron-right` icon. In the first item, we added the `.active` class, which turned this item blue and changed the colors of both the text and the icon.

This is almost awesome! It just needs some adjustments in the CSS to look perfect. Let's use some :nth-child selectors to style some elements based on their position, such as the first item in the menu (:first-child) and the last item (:last-child). Add the following CSS:

```
#profile-settings .nav-stacked li {
    border-bottom: 1px solid #e5e5e5;
    margin: 0;
}

#profile-settings .nav-stacked a {
    border-radius: 0;
}

#profile-settings .nav-stacked li:first-child a {
    border-radius: 0.4rem 0.4rem 0 0;
}

#profile-settings .nav-stacked li:last-child {
    border-bottom: 0;
}

#profile-settings .nav-stacked li:last-child a {
    border-radius: 0 0 0.4rem 0.4rem;
}
```

We just removed unwanted margins and the border radius, while adding a border bottom to all elements in the list, except the last one. This is because of the #profile-settings .nav-stacked li:last-child selector, where we a specific rule only for the last item element.

We also changed border-radius for the first element and the last element to create a rounded border in the pill list. The .nav-pill menu will appear like what is shown in the next screenshot:

Tabs in the middle

In the #main column, we must create a tab option with the settings content. Bootstrap also offers a tabs component with the navigation components. First, we will work with the markup and CSS style and use it with JavaScript.

Therefore, inside the #main tag, place the following markup, corresponding to the Bootstrap tabs:

```
<ul id="account-tabs" class="nav nav-tabs nav-justified">
  <li role="presentation" class="active">
    <a href="#account-user">User info</a>
  </li>
  <li role="presentation">
    <a href="#account-language">Language</a>
  </li>
  <li role="presentation">
    <a href="#account-mobile">Mobile</a>
  </li>
</ul>
```

Just like the Pills, to use tabs, create a list with the `.nav` and `.nav-tabs` classes. We used the `.nav-justified` class as well to make the tabs equally distributed over the component.

Moreover, we populated the list with some items. Each link of the item contains an identifier, which will be used to link each tab to the corresponding content. Keep that information at the moment.

Let's add some CSS rules to keep the same border colors that we are using:

```
#account-tabs > li {
    border-bottom: 0.1rem solid #e5e5e5;
}

#account-tabs a {
    border-bottom: 0;
}

#account-tabs li.active {
    border-bottom: 0;
}
```

Refresh the web page and you should see it like this:

Adding the tab content

To add the tab content, we use the named *tab panes*. Each tab must be placed in an element with the `.tab-pane` class and have the corresponding identifier in the *tab* component. After the tab list, add the HTML code for the tab panes:

```
<ul id="account-tabs" class="nav nav-tabs nav-justified">
  <li role="presentation" class="active">
    <a href="#account-user">User info</a>
  </li>
  <li role="presentation">
    <a href="#account-language">Language</a>
  </li>
  <li role="presentation">
    <a href="#account-mobile">Mobile</a>
  </li>
</ul>

<div class="tab-content">
  <div role="tabpanel" class="tab-pane active" id="account-user">
    User info tab pane
  </div>
  <div role="tabpanel" class="tab-pane" id="account-language">
    Language tab pane
  </div>
  <div role="tabpanel" class="tab-pane" id="account-mobile">
    Mobile tab pane
  </div>
</div>
```

Refresh the web page and you will see only the content of `#account-user` appearing, although clicking on other tabs will not cause any switch between them. This is because we have not initialized the component through JavaScript yet.

Using the Bootstrap tabs plugin

We can initialize the tabs with simple JavaScript code, like what is presented next. However, we will do that in a smarter way using data markup:

```
$('#account-tabs a').click(function (e) {
  e.preventDefault()
  $(this).tab('show')
})
```

For data markup, we must add the `data-toggle="tab"` attribute on the link elements, inside the list. Change the list markup for the following:

```
<ul id="account-tabs" class="nav nav-tabs nav-justified">
  <li role="presentation" class="active">
    <a href="#account-user" data-toggle="tab">User info</a>
  </li>
  <li role="presentation">
    <a href="#account-language" data-toggle="tab">Language</a>
  </li>
  <li role="presentation">
    <a href="#account-mobile" data-toggle="tab">Mobile</a>
  </li>
</ul>
```

 If you are using pills, add the `data-toggle="pill"` attribute, just as we did for tabs.

Refresh the web browser and switch between the tabs. It works like a charm! To make it even fancier, add the `.fade` class to each `.tab-pane` to create a fade effect when changing tabs.

Creating content in the user info tab

Inside the `.tab-pane` identified by `#account-user`, let's add some content. Since it is a configuration menu, we will create a form to set the user settings. Again, we will work with some forms in Bootstrap. Do you remember how to use them?

In the form, we will have three inputs (name, username, and e-mail) followed by a button to save the changes. We will use the `.form-horizontal` class to make each form input next its label and stacked by each other. So, place the following code inside the `#account-user` element:

```
<div id="account-user" role="tabpanel" class="tab-pane active" >
  <form class="form-horizontal">
    <div class="form-group">
      <label class="col-sm-3 control-label">Name</label>
      <div class="col-sm-9">
        <input type="text" class="form-control" value="Jonny Doo">
      </div>
```

```
      </div>
      <div class="form-group">
        <label class="col-sm-3 control-label">Username</label>
        <div class="col-sm-9">
          <div class="input-group">
            <div class="input-group-addon">@</div>
            <input type="text" class="form-control"
value="jonnydoo">
          </div>
        </div>
      </div>
      <div class="form-group">
        <label class="col-sm-3 control-label">Email</label>
        <div class="col-sm-9">
          <input type="email" class="form-control"
value="jonnydoo@dogmail.com">
        </div>
      </div>
      <div class="form-group">
        <div class="col-sm-offset-3 col-sm-9">
          <button type="submit" class="btn btn-primary">
            Save changes
          </button>
        </div>
      </div>
    </form>
</div>
```

Break through the code, we set the labels to fill a quarter of the form row, while the input fills the rest. We again used the input groups to add the @ sign before the username field.

Each label has the .col-sm-3 class and the input the .col-sm-9 class. As we said, the forms respect the grid system layout, so we can apply the same classes here. We also added the .col-sm-offset-3 class to the submit button for a correct offset.

Right now, the page should look like the following screenshot. Isn't it looking nicer?

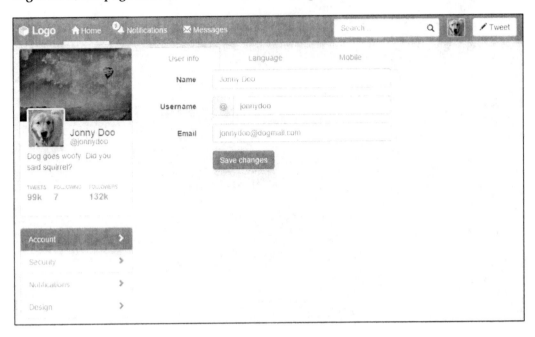

CSS turn! We must make it look prettier, so let's play with some paddings. However, before anything, add the class to `.card` to the `.tab-content`. Next, let's fix the borders and margins in `.tab-content` by adding some padding and some negative margin, as follows:

```
#main .tab-content {
  padding: 2em;
  margin-top: -0.1rem;
}
```

Then, remove the border from the tab list and change the z-index of the tabs:

```
#account-tabs > li {
  border-bottom: 0;
}

#account-tabs {
  position: relative;
  z-index: 99;
}
```

Finally, remove the margin from the save changes button using another `nth` recipe, as follows:

```
#main .form-horizontal .form-group:last-child {
  margin-bottom: 0;
}
```

Nice! Refresh the web app and see the result, like this:

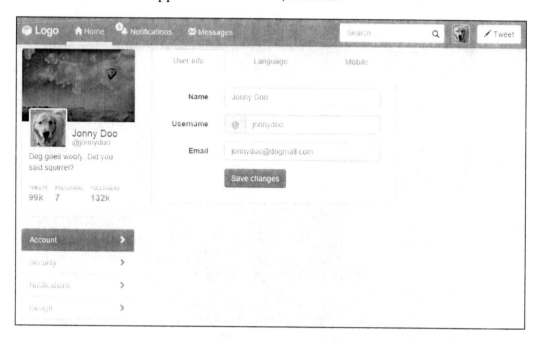

With these changes, we have made the form from `.tab-content` look like a card. We also added some margins and padding to correct the designs. Lastly, with the margin top and z-index, we make the selected tab blend correctly with the content.

The stats column

To finalize the settings page, we must fill the right column of the web app. To do this, we will create a menu that presents some general statistics about the user.

In order to do that, we will use the Bootstrap List group component. List group is powerful in Bootstrap as it can seem similar to Bootstrap Cards, but it has more specific options for menu list generation, such as headers, disabled items, and much more.

So let's start doing this! Create the HTML markup at the `#right-content` element:

```
<div id="right-content" class="col-md-3 hidden-sm hidden-xs">
  <ul class="list-group">
    <li class="list-group-item list-group-item-info">
      Dog stats
    </li>
    <li class="list-group-item">
      Number of day rides
    </li>
    <li class="list-group-item">
      Captured mice
    </li>
    <li class="list-group-item">
      Postmen frightened
    </li>
    <li class="list-group-item">
      Always alert badge
    </li>
  </ul>
</div>
```

It is a simple list and we just added the `.list-group` class to the list, while adding the `.list-group-item` class for each item in the list. For the first item, we used the `.list-group-item-info` contextual color class to make it blue, according to the Bootstrap contextual colors.

Before we continue, we have to change the colors of the borders from list group to respect the same border color that we have been using:

```
.list-group-item {
  border-color: #e5e5e5;
}
```

The result that you should see right know is like the one presented in the next screenshot. List groups is a very handy component that we can use to achieve almost the same effect that we got using Pills, but here we are using fewer CSS rules.

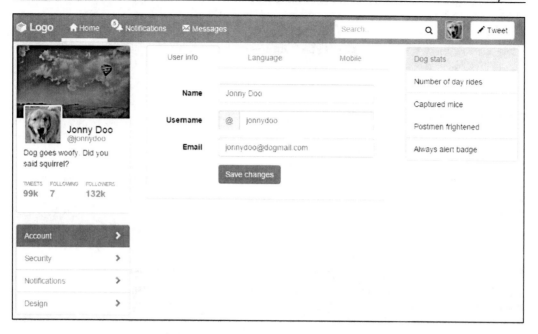

Labels and badges

Labels and badges are Bootstrap components that can easily highlight some text or information. They can be used in any place, as we did in the navigation bar, on the notification item.

Just like most of Bootstrap's components, labels follow the contextual colors of Bootstrap, while badges do not have this option. To consolidate their utilization, let's add some of them to the right menu, regarding the statistics, because after all we want to know our stats!

It will be pretty easy since we have worked with this before. For the three first items, we will use labels, and for the last one, we will use a badge with an icon. Just add the highlighted code to the current `.list-group`:

```
<div id="right-content" class="col-md-3 hidden-sm hidden-xs">
  <ul class="list-group">
    <li class="list-group-item list-group-item-info">
      Dog stats
    </li>
    <li class="list-group-item">
      Number of day rides
      <span class="label label-success">3</span>
    </li>
```

```
      <li class="list-group-item">
        Captured mice
        <span class="label label-danger">87</span>
      </li>
      <li class="list-group-item">
        Postmen frightened
        <span class="label label-default">2</span>
      </li>
      <li class="list-group-item">
        Always alert badge
        <span class="badge glyphicon glyphicon-star" aria-hidden="true">
        </span>
      </li>
    </ul>
  </div>
```

We must pay attention to some points here. The first is that we used the .label class together with the contextual color class, like this: .label-*. Here, * is the name of the contextual class.

The second thing is that if you refresh your web page right now, you will see that Bootstrap does have a CSS for aligning all badges on the right, but it does not apply the same rule for labels. So, add the next CSS:

```
#right-content .list-group .label {
  float: right;
}
```

The third point is that we used badges and icons in the same span. This is possible, and then we just need to adjust the CSS render:

```
#right-content .list-group .label {
  padding: 0.3rem 0.6rem;
}


#right-content .list-group .badge.glyphicon-star {
  background-color: #f0ad4e;
  padding: 0.4rem;
  padding-left: 0.5rem;
}
```

By adding these rules, we adjusted the padding for the labels, adjusted the padding for the badge, and correctly set the yellow background for the star badge. See the result in the browser; it must look like this:

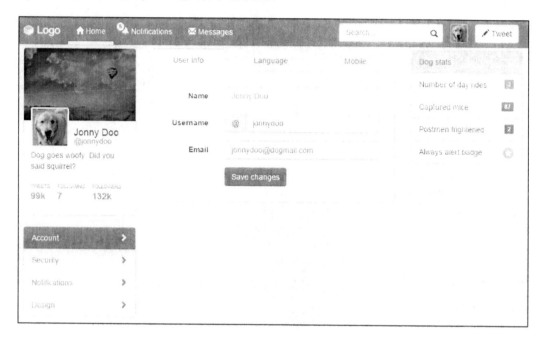

Cool! We've done another page for our web app. The stats menu looks cute. We will not cover the other page settings menus in this book, since they follow almost the same structure that we showed in this example. Try doing that as homework.

Summary

In this chapter, we covered a bunch of Bootstrap components. Now you can say that you know all of the most important Bootstrap components, even the new ones in version 4. This chapter was a challenging one, since you had to learn so many details about different components, so congratulations!

First, we started working with alerts. We only used the component alert with data attributes, but in the coming chapters, we will use it as a JavaScript plugin, with more options and animations. Don't worry! This is a glimpse of future chapters.

Next, you learned about progress bars and made use of some customization, and using animations by CSS. With that, we achieved a cool result at the end and are now able to use progress bars when needed.

After that, we switched to the settings page. There, taking advantage of the same web application structure, we changed the layout. We did this by creating a menu using the pills navigator, and created a main component that used tabs.

For tabs, that was the first time we presented how to use a Bootstrap plugin by using JavaScript, but do not worry about this either. We will go deep into this subject in the next chapter.

To finish the chapter, we worked with other component, called list group. This component offers some more capabilities for creating stacked menus.

Inside the items, we studied the use of labels and badges, which are nice things that Bootstrap offers to us.

In the next chapter, we will start working with some Bootstrap JavaScript plugins. We will go back to the main web application page and play with some posts on the timeline. It will be fun. See you there!

8

Working with JavaScript

The whole Internet would not have been the same without JavaScript, and so is Bootstrap. The JavaScript plugins from Bootstrap account for a chunk of Bootstrap's success. By having them, Bootstrap has allowed all of us to use modals, alerts, tooltips, and other plugins out of the box.

Therefore, the main focus of this chapter is to explain the main Bootstrap JavaScript plugins by using them in our web application. In the previous chapters, we used a few plugins. The purpose of this chapter is to go deep into this subject. The key points that we will cover now are:

- General usage of Bootstrap JavaScript plugins
- Data attributes
- Modals
- Tooltips
- Popover
- Affix

Understanding JavaScript plugins

As I said, Bootstrap offers a lot of JavaScript plugins. They all come together when we download the framework, and all of them are ready for use when the `bootstrap.js` file is loaded in HTML, although each plugin can be downloaded individually as well from the Bootstrap website.

Minifying JavaScript

In the production stage, you can use the minified version of Bootstrap JavaScript. We are not using that right now for learning purposes, but it is recommended that you use the minimal version when you go live.

The library dependencies

While we were setting up our development environment, we spoke about the need to import the jQuery library. Actually, jQuery is now the only required external dependency for Bootstrap.

Check out the `bower.json` file in the Bootstrap repository for further information about dependencies.

Bower

Bower is a package management control system for client-side components. To use Bower, you must have both Node and npm installed. Bower was developed by the developers of Twitter.

Data attributes

HTML5 introduced the idea of adding custom attributes to document tags in order to store custom information. Therefore, you can add an attribute to a tag with the `data-*` prefix, retrieve the information in JavaScript, and not get started with some plugin in your browser. An overwhelming majority of web browsers do support the use of custom data attributes.

With that ideology, Bootstrap implemented all the plugins to be used with just data attributes. This goes towards the framework idea to increase the speed of development and prototyping. This is because you can make use of plugins without typing JavaScript code.

To control that methodology, Bootstrap implemented an API so that you can access all plugins through only data attributes. Sometimes, however, you may want to turn off access through the API. To do so, insert the following command at the beginning of your JavaScript code:

```
$(document).off('.data-api');
```

To disable the API for some specific plugins, prepend the plugin namespace. For instance, to disable the alerts API, type this:

```
$(document).off('.alert.data-api');
```

Bootstrap JavaScript events

There is a set of events that Bootstrap produces for each plugin. They are triggered usually before and after the event starts. To exemplify this, let's say that we have a Bootstrap modal (you will learn about using modals in this chapter; don't worry) and we will call it to open by JavaScript:

```
$('#some-modal').modal();
```

When this happens, Bootstrap triggers the events called show.bs.modal and shown.bs.modal. The first one is called before the *open modal* call and the other is called after the action. Let's say we want to customize our modal before it is shown. To do this, we must use the first event:

```
$('#some-modal').on('shown.bs.modal', function(e) {
  // do some customization before shown
});
```

The events can be used for all plugins. Just change the namespace (in this case, .modal is the namespace) to achieve the result.

Awesome Bootstrap modals

It's time to learn how to use modals! Modals are really present nowadays in web development and Bootstrap plugins, for that is really complete and easy to use. To use it, let's go back to our main web application page, the one containing the feeds.

First, we add the .hide helper class to the div.alert that we created at the #main column. We will play with alerts later. Now, go to the #tweet button on the navigation bar. We want to open a modal for tweets when clicking on this button. So, add the markup to the element:

```
<!-- modal launch button -->
<button id="tweet" class="btn btn-default pull-right visible-xs-block"
data-toggle="modal" data-target="#tweet-modal">
  <span class="glyphicon glyphicon-pencil" aria-hidden="true"></span>
  Tweet
</button>
```

What we did is the call to open a modal, recognized by the #tweet-modal ID and the data-toggle="modal" data attribute. We could also have done that via JavaScript with this code:

```
$('#tweet-modal').modal();
```

Create the modal by adding the next HTML code. We have created all the modals at the end of our HTML code, outside of all Bootstrap elements and right before the loading of the JavaScript libraries:

```
<div class="modal fade" id="tweet-modal" tabindex="-1"
role="dialog">
  <div class="modal-dialog" role="document">
    <div class="modal-content">
      <div class="modal-header">
        <button type="button" class="close" data-dismiss="modal"
aria-label="Close">
          <span aria-hidden="true">&times;</span>
        </button>
        <h4 class="modal-title">Modal title</h4>
      </div>
      <div class="modal-body">
        Modal content
      </div>
      <div class="modal-footer">
        <button type="button" class="btn btn-default" data-
dismiss="modal">
          Close
        </button>
        <button type="button" class="btn btn-primary">
          Save changes
        </button>
      </div>
    </div>
  </div>
</div>
```

Reload the web application, click on the **Tweet** button and see the magic happen! This code is a little more complex, so let's explain each part separately. The following screenshot shows what the first draft of our modal looks like. Now let's understand what we did.

Modal general and content

The first tag used to initiate a modal is a `<div>` with the `.modal` class. Note that we also added the `.fade` class to create the effect of fade in and fade out when the modal appears and disappears.

Inside the `.modal` element, we created two more nested tags. The first one is `.modal-dialog`, which will wrap all of the modal dialog. Inside it, we created `.modal-content`, which will hold the content of the modal itself.

The modal header

Next, inside `.modal-content` we have the `.modal-header` element. In the modal header, we can add some title information about the modal. In our example, we have also added a close button that hides the modal using a `data-dismiss="modal"` data attribute.

The modal body

The modal body is where you should place the main content of the modal. A cool feature inside the modal is the ability to use scaffolding.

To use the grid system inside the modal body, you do not need to create a container. Just create a `.row` inside `.modal-body` and start adding columns, as shown in the following example in bold:

```
<div class="modal fade" id="tweet-modal" tabindex="-1"
role="dialog">
  <div class="modal-dialog" role="document">
    <div class="modal-content">
      <div class="modal-header">
        <button type="button" class="close" data-dismiss="modal"
aria-label="Close">
          <span aria-hidden="true">&times;</span>
        </button>
        <h4 class="modal-title">Modal title</h4>
      </div>
      <div class="modal-body">
        <div class="row">
          <div class="col-sm-2">Use</div>
          <div class="col-sm-4">the</div>
          <div class="col-sm-6">grid system</div>
        </div>
      </div>
      <div class="modal-footer">
        <button type="button" class="btn btn-default" data-
dismiss="modal">
          Close
        </button>
        <button type="button" class="btn btn-primary">
          Save changes
        </button>
      </div>
    </div>
  </div>
</div>
```

The modal footer

At the end of the modal, you can create a `.modal-footer` element to place some other components, such as buttons, as we did in the previous example.

Creating our custom modal

Now that you have learned how to use a Bootstrap modal, let's customize it for our example. First, let's add some content inside our `.modal-body` and edit `.modal-header` and `.modal-footer` a little:

```
<div class="modal fade" id="tweet-modal" tabindex="-1"
role="dialog">
  <div class="modal-dialog" role="document">
    <div class="modal-content">
      <div class="modal-header">
        <button type="button" class="close" data-dismiss="modal"
aria-label="Close">
          <span aria-hidden="true">&times;</span>
        </button>
        <h4 class="modal-title">Dog a new tweet</h4>
      </div>
      <div class="modal-body">
        <textarea class="form-control" rows="4" placeholder="What you
want to bark?" maxlength="140"></textarea>
      </div>
      <div class="modal-footer">
        <span class="char-count pull-left" data-max="140">140</span>
        <button type="button" class="btn btn-default" data-
dismiss="modal">
          Close
        </button>
        <button type="button" class="btn btn-primary">
          Tweet
        </button>
      </div>
    </div>
  </div>
</div>
```

Here, we added a heading to `.modal-header`, a textarea in `.modal-body` and a `<span>` element with the `.char-count` class in the footer.

The goal here is to type a tweet inside the `textarea` element and update the character count in the footer to show how many characters are left for the user to enter.

For styling, go to the CSS and add a style rule for `.char-count`:

```
#tweet-modal .char-count {
    padding: 0.7rem 0;
}
```

Refresh the web browser and see the result of the tweet modal, as shown in the following screenshot. Now, we need to add some JavaScript to count the number of remaining characters to tweet.

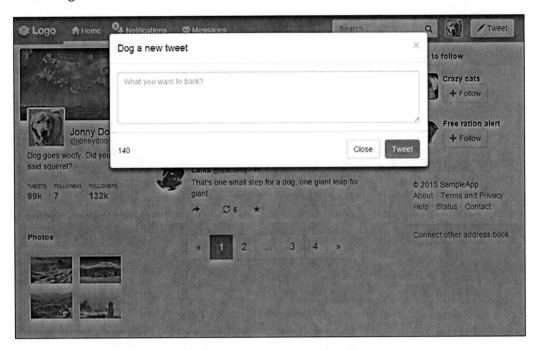

So, for the JavaScript for the character count, open (or create it if you do not have it yet) the `main.js` file. Ensure that you have the document ready to create the script, by having the following code in your file:

```
$(document).ready(function() {
    // add code here
});
```

Then, we must create a function that updates the remaining characters each time a letter is typed. Therefore, let's create an event handler for `keyup`.

The `keyup` event came from jQuery, which has a lot of event handlers that are triggered on different actions. There are also other events such as `click`, `hover`, and so on. In this case, `keyup` will trigger when you release a key that you pressed.

The basic usage to create a bind event is from a selector, call the .on function passing at the first argument of the event type (in this case, `keyup`), followed by the handler (in our case, a function). Here, we have presented the JavaScript code, and the event handler is in bold so as to highlight the usage:

```
$(document).ready(function() {
    var $charCount, maxCharCount;

    $charCount = $('#tweet-modal .char-count')
    maxCharCount = parseInt($charCount.data('max'), 10);

    $('#tweet-modal textarea').on('keyup', function(e) {
        var tweetLength = $(e.currentTarget).val().length;

        $charCount.html(maxCharCount - tweetLength);
    });
});
```

 We used the `keyup` event handler to trigger the event after the key is released and the character is typed. Therefore, the new length of `textarea` is already computed when we make a comparison.

A tool for your tip

Tooltips are a very useful component for describing in detail an element or a web page. For example, when you have an image and want to describe it further, you add a tooltip. When users hover over the image, they see further information.

In our case, we will use tooltips for the buttons present in every tweet, such as `Reply`, `Retweet`, and `Start`. This Bootstrap plugin component is pretty simple and useful in many cases. To start it, just add the markup in bold to the tweets in the middle column (`<li>` in the `ul#feed` element):

```
<ul id="feed" class="list-unstyled">
  <li>
    <img src="imgs/doge.jpg" class="feed-avatar img-circle">
    <div class="feed-post">
```

```html
        <h5>Doge <small>@dogeoficial - 3h</small></h5>
        <p>You can't hold a dog down without staying down with
him!</p>
    </div>
    <div class="action-list">
        <a href="#" data-toggle="tooltip" data-placement="bottom"
title="Reply">
            <span class="glyphicon glyphicon-share-alt" aria-
hidden="true"></span>
        </a>
        <a href="#" data-toggle="tooltip" data-placement="bottom"
title="Retweet">
            <span class="glyphicon glyphicon-refresh" aria-
hidden="true"></span>
            <span class="retweet-count">6</span>
        </a>
        <a href="#" data-toggle="tooltip" data-placement="bottom"
title="Start">
            <span class="glyphicon glyphicon-star" aria-hidden="true"></
span>
        </a>
    </div>
  </li>

  <li>
    <img src="imgs/laika.jpg" class="feed-avatar img-circle">
    <div class="feed-post">
      <h5>Laika <small>@spacesog - 4h</small></h5>
      <p>That's one small step for a dog, one giant leap for
giant</p>
    </div>
    <div class="action-list">
        <a href="#" data-toggle="tooltip" data-placement="bottom"
title="Reply">
            <span class="glyphicon glyphicon-share-alt" aria-
hidden="true"></span>
        </a>
        <a href="#" data-toggle="tooltip" data-placement="bottom"
title="Retweet">
            <span class="glyphicon glyphicon-refresh" aria-
hidden="true"></span>
            <span class="retweet-count">6</span>
        </a>
        <a href="#" data-toggle="tooltip" data-placement="bottom"
title="Star">
```

```
        <span class="glyphicon glyphicon-star" aria-hidden="true"></
span>
      </a>
    </div>
  </li>
</ul>
```

As you can notice, by using data attributes, you just need to add three of them to make a tooltip. The first one is `data-toggle`, which says the type of toggle. In our case, it is `tooltip`. The `data-placement` attribute is concerned with the placement of the tooltip (obviously). In this case, we set it to appear at the bottom, but we can set it to `left`, `top`, `bottom`, `right`, or `auto`. Finally, we add the `title` attribute, which is not a data attribute, because HTML already has the attribute title, so we can call it by this attribute.

Refresh the web app in the browser, hover the icon and you will see that... nothing happens! Unlike the other plugins, the tooltip and popover Bootstrap plugins cannot be activated simply through data attributes. They did this because of some issues, so it must be initialized through a JavaScript command. Therefore, add the following line to the `main.js` file:

```
$(document).ready(function() {
    ... // to rest of the code
    $('[data-toggle="tooltip"]').tooltip();
});
```

The `[data-toggle="tooltip"]` selector will retrieve all the tooltip elements and start it. You can also pass some options inside while calling the `.tooltip()` start function. The next table shows some main options (to see all of them, refer to the official documentation of Bootstrap) that can be passed through JavaScript or data attributes:

Option	Type	Default	Description
`animation`	Boolean	`true`	This adds fade in and fade out animation to a tooltip.
`placement`	String or function	`top`	This is the placement position of the tooltip. The options are the same as those mentioned for the usage with data attributes (`top`, `bottom`, `left`, `right`, and `auto`). You can pass `auto` with another option, such as `auto left`, which will always show the tooltip on the left as long as it is possible, and then show it on the right.
`selector`	String	`false`	If you provide a selector, the tooltip will be delegated to the specified target.

Option	Type	Default	Description
`trigger`	String	`hover` `focus`	The trigger to the tooltip will be shown. The options are `click`, `hover`, `focus`, and `manual`. You can pass multiple options for trigger, unless you use `manual`, in which case you need to write a function to activate the plugin.

The tooltip plugin also has some useful methods for doing things such as showing all tooltips. You can call them using the `.tooltip()` method. As mentioned, if you want to show all tooltips, just use `$('.tooltip-selector').tooltip('show')`. The other options are `hide`, `toggle`, and `destroy`.

Pop it all over

In some cases, you may want to show more information that does not fit in a simple tooltip component. For that, Bootstrap has created popovers, which are components that create small overlays of content to show detailed secondary information.

The popover plugin is an extension of the tooltip plugin, so if you are using separate plugins, you must load both to make it work. Also, just like tooltips, popovers cannot be activated simply through data attributes. You must call them via JavaScript to make them work.

Let's use a popover in our web app example, on the right-hand-side column, the one identified by `div#who-follow`. We will add the popover to the **Follow** buttons, and for that, we need to do two things. The first one is to change the `<button>` element to an `<a>` element and then add the popover markup.

Why do we need to change buttons to links in popover?

Actually, we don't have to change the buttons' markup; we will do that just because of cross-browser compatibility. There are some browsers that do not support all the functionalities, such as the click **Dismiss** option present in the popover.

First, about the `<buttons>` inside the `div#who-follow` element. Change them to `<a>` elements in the HTML. Also add the `role="button"` and `tabindex="-1"` attributes to the links to fix the issue of cross-browser compatibility:

```
<div id="who-follow" class="card">
  <div class="card-header">
    Who to follow
  </div>
```

```
<div class="card-block">
  <ul class="list-unstyled">
    <li>
      <img src="imgs/cat.jpg" class="img-rounded">
      <div class="info">
        <strong>Crazy cats</strong>
        <a href="#" role="button" tabindex="-1" class="btn btn-
default">
          <span class="glyphicon glyphicon-plus" aria-
hidden="true"></span> Follow
        </a>
      </div>
    </li>
    <li>
      <img src="imgs/ration.jpg" class="img-rounded">
      <div class="info">
        <strong>Free ration alert</strong>
        <a href="#" role="button" tabindex="-1" class="btn btn-
default">
          <span class="glyphicon glyphicon-plus" aria-
hidden="true"></span> Follow
        </a>
      </div>
    </li>
  </ul>
</div>
```

The code in bold refers to the changes from button to link. Now, we must add the popover markup. It is pretty simple and follows most of the data attributes presented in the tooltip plugin:

```
<div id="who-follow" class="card">
  <div class="card-header">
    Who to follow
  </div>
  <div class="card-block">
    <ul class="list-unstyled">
      <li>
        <img src="imgs/cat.jpg" class="img-rounded">
        <div class="info">
          <strong>Crazy cats</strong>
          <a href="#" role="button" tabindex="-1" class="btn btn-
default" data-toggle="popover" data-trigger="focus" title="You may
want to follow">
```

```
                <span class="glyphicon glyphicon-plus" aria-
hidden="true"></span> Follow
            </a>
          </div>
        </li>
        <li>
          <img src="imgs/ration.jpg" class="img-rounded">
          <div class="info">
            <strong>Free ration alert</strong>
            <a href="#" role="button" tabindex="-1" class="btn btn-
default" data-toggle="popover" data-trigger="focus" title="You may
want to follow">
              <span class="glyphicon glyphicon-plus" aria-
hidden="true"></span> Follow
            </a>
          </div>
        </li>
      </ul>
    </div>
```

Just like the popover, add the following line to the JavaScript code to make popovers appear:

```
$(document).ready(function() {
    … // the rest of the JavaScript
    $('[data-toggle="popover"]').popover();
});
```

Refresh the web browser, click on the **Follow** button and see the popover appearing to the right of the button. Now we will make some changes using the options to customize it. First of all, let's create the content that will appear inside the popover and change its placement in JavaScript:

```
$(document).ready(function() {
    … // rest of the JavaScript
    var popoverContentTemplate = '' +
        '<img src="imgs/breed.jpg" class="img-rounded">' +
        '<div class="info">' +
            '<strong>Dog Breeds</strong>' +
            '<a href="#" class="btn btn-default">' +
                '<span class="glyphicon glyphicon-plus" aria-
hidden="true"></span>' +
                'Follow' +
            '</a>' +
        '</div>';
```

```
$('[data-toggle="popover"]').popover({
    placement: 'bottom',
    html: true,
    content: function() {
        return popoverContentTemplate;
    }
});
});
```

In the preceding code, we changed the placement of the popover to `bottom` and set the content that will appear inside the popover to be HTML with the `html: true` option. The content was provided by a function that simply returned the `popoverContentTemplate` variable.

For instance, we could have used the template in very different ways that are more optimized, but we did this to show the method of adding HTML content onto a popover via JavaScript and using a function for that. We could have called and used some options of the target clicked button inside the function by accessing the current scope in the `this` variable.

Popover events

Popovers and tooltips provide some nice events. As was said before, Bootstrap triggers some events when plugin elements appear, hide, and are inserted. To play with these, let's use the `show.bs.popover` event, which is an event that is fired immediately when the `popover` is `show`. In this case, we want to create an action before the `popover` is `show`. We want to change the text of the **Follow** button that we clicked on to **Following**, while changing the icon next to the text from a plus sign to an okay sign. We can take advantage of the `show.bs.popover` Bootstrap event to make these changes. In the JavaScript file, insert the following delegation to the popovers:

```
$(document).ready(function() {
    ... // the rest of the JavaScript code
    $('[data-toggle="popover"]').on('show.bs.popover', function()
{
        var $icon = $(this).find('span.glyphicon');

        $icon.removeClass('glyphicon-plus').addClass('glyphicon-ok');
        $(this).append('ing');
    });
});
```

The scope of this event is the element of `data-toggle`, which is the **Follow** button. We query the icon inside the button, and change it from `glyphicon-plus` to `glyphicon-ok`. Finally, we append the infinitive `ing` to **Follow**, which means that we are now following **Crazy cats** or **Free ration alert** suggestions:

To add a cherry to the pie, let's change the color of the icon from blue to green when the okay icon appears:

```
div#who-follow li .info .glyphicon-ok {
    color: #5cb85c;
}
```

Refresh the web browser and click on the **Follow** button. You should see something similar to this screenshot:

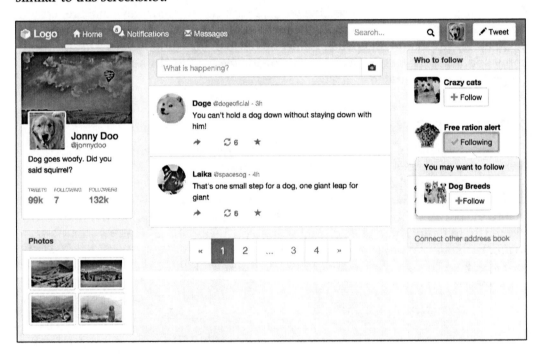

There are many other places where the Bootstrap events can be used. This is a nice example where we want to change the element that we are interacting with. Keep in mind to change it whenever you need some related interaction.

Making the menu affix

The affix plugin is present only in version 3 of Bootstrap (it was removed in version 4), and it aims to toggle the position of an element between fixed and relative, emulating the effect of position: sticky, which is not present in all browsers.

We will apply the sticky effect the left #profile element although we do not have enough elements to make a scroll on our web page. Therefore, to make it simple, replicate the <li> in ul#feed to increase the number of items in the list. Do this three times or more to make a scroll in your web browser.

In div#profile, add the markup related to affix:

```
<div id="profile" class="col-md-3 hidden-sm hidden-xs" data-
spy="affix" data-offset-top="0">
    …
    // rest of the profile HTML
</div>
```

Refresh the web browser. You will see that the affix is not working yet. Since we are making the left column with a fixed position with the affix plugin, it is removing the entire column from the grid, making the columns glitch from left to right.

So, we need a workaround for that. We must create some piece of JavaScript code using the events triggered for the plugin.

Let's use the affix.bs.affix event, which is an event fired just before the affixing of the element:

```
$(document).ready(function() {
    … // rest of the JavaScript code

    $('#profile').on('affix.bs.affix', function() {
        $(this).width($(this).width() - 1);
        $('#main').addClass('col-md-offset-3');
    }).on('affix-top.bs.affix', function() {
        $(this).css('width', '');
        $('#main').removeClass('col-md-offset-3');
    });
});
```

Thus, we have played with some tricks in the preceding JavaScript code.

In the first delegated event, .on('affix.bs.affix', handler),when the element switches to position: fixed, we keep the width of the left column. It would change the width because the .col-md-3 class does not have a fixed width; it uses a percentage width.

We also added the offset to the middle column, corresponding to the detached left column, the `.col-md-offset-3` class.

The `affix-top.bs.affix` event does the opposite action, firing when the element returns to the original top position and removing the custom width and the offset class in the middle column.

To remove the fixed width and return to the `.col-md-3` percentage width, just add the `$(this).css('width', '')` line. Also remove the `.col-md-offset-3` class from the `#main` content.

Refresh the web browser, scroll the page, and see the result, exemplified in the next screenshot. Note that the profile is fixed on the left while the rest of the content scrolls with the page:

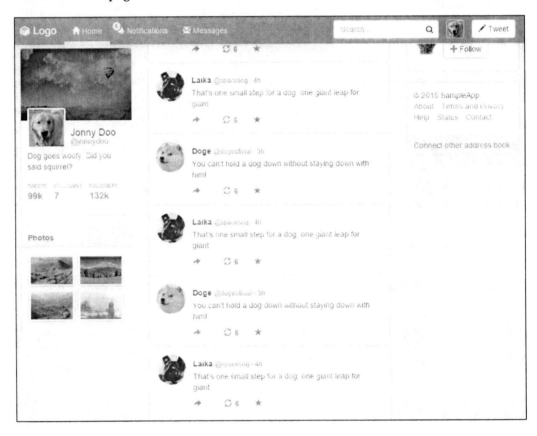

Finishing the web app

To finish the web application example, we just need to create another modal when we click on the **Messages** link at the navigation bar.

To create it, we will use the same methodology used to create the modal for the **Tweet** button. So, add the data attributes' markups to the **Messages** link in .nav. navbar-nav, as follows:

```
<ul class="nav navbar-nav">
  <li class="active">
    <a href="#">
      <span class="glyphicon glyphicon-home" aria-hidden="true"></
span>
      Home
    </a>
  </li>
  <li>
    <a href="#">
      <span class="badge">5</span>
      <span class="glyphicon glyphicon-bell" aria-hidden="true"></
span>
      Notifications
    </a>
  </li>
  <li>
    <a href="#" role="button" data-toggle="modal" data-
target="#messages-modal">
      <span class="glyphicon glyphicon-envelope" aria-hidden="true"></
span>
      Messages
    </a>
  </li>
  <li class="visible-xs-inline">
    <a href="#">
      <span class="glyphicon glyphicon-user" aria-hidden="true"></
span>
      Profile
    </a>
  </li>
  <li class="visible-xs-inline">
```

```
        <a href="#">
          <span class="glyphicon glyphicon-off" aria-hidden="true"></span>
          Logout
        </a>
      </li>
    </ul>
```

The highlighted code says that this link plays the `role` button, toggling a modal identified by the `#messages-modal` ID. Create the base of this modal at the end of the HTML code, just after `#tweet-modal`:

```
<div id="messages-modal" class="modal fade" tabindex="-1"
role="dialog">
  <div class="modal-dialog" role="document">
    <div class="modal-content">
      <div class="modal-header">
        <button type="button" class="close" data-dismiss="modal"
aria-label="Close">
          <span aria-hidden="true">&times;</span>
        </button>
        <h4 class="modal-title">Dog messages</h4>
        <button type="button" class="btn btn-primary btn-message">New
message</button>
      </div>
      <div class="modal-body">
      </div>
    </div>
  </div>
</div>
```

We made some changes in comparison to `#tweet-modal`. Firstly, we removed `.modal-footer` from this modal, since we do not need these options in the modal. Like almost the entire framework, Bootstrap allows us to include or exclude elements as per our wishes.

Secondly, we created a new button, **New message**, in the header, identified by the `.btn-message` class. To present the button correctly, create the following CSS style:

```
#messages-modal .btn-message {
  position: absolute;
  right: 3em;
  top: 0.75em;
}
```

Now let's create the content inside the modal. We will add a list of messages in the modal. Check out the HTML with the content added:

```html
<div class="modal fade" id="messages-modal" tabindex="-1"
role="dialog">
  <div class="modal-dialog" role="document">
    <div class="modal-content">
      <div class="modal-header">
        <button type="button" class="close" data-dismiss="modal"
aria-label="Close">
          <span aria-hidden="true">&times;</span>
        </button>
        <h4 class="modal-title">Dog messages</h4>
        <button type="button" class="btn btn-primary btn-message">New
message</button>
      </div>
      <div class="modal-body">
        <ul class="list-unstyled">
          <li>
            <a href="#">
              <img src="imgs/laika.jpg" class="img-circle">
              <div class="msg-content">
                <h5>Laika <small>@spacesog</small></h5>
                <p>Hey Jonny, how is down there?</p>
              </div>
            </a>
          </li>
          <li>
            <a href="#">
              <img src="imgs/doge.jpg" class="img-circle">
              <div class="msg-content">
                <h5>Doge <small>@dogeoficial </small></h5>
                <p>Wow! How did I turned in to a meme?</p>
              </div>
            </a>
          </li>
          <li>
            <a href="#">
              <img src="imgs/cat.jpg" class="img-circle">
              <div class="msg-content">
                <h5>Cat <small>@crazycat</small></h5>
                <p>You will never catch me!</p>
              </div>
```

```
            </a>
          </li>
          <li>
            <a href="#">
              <img src="imgs/laika.jpg" class="img-circle">
              <div class="msg-content">
                <h5>Laika <small>@spacesog</small></h5>
                <p>I think I saw you in Jupiter! Have you been there
recently?</p>
              </div>
            </a>
          </li>
        </ul>
      </div>
    </div>
  </div>
</div>
```

To finish our job, we just create some style in the CSS in order to display our list correctly:

```css
#messages-modal .modal-body {
  max-height: 32rem;
  overflow: auto;
}

#messages-modal li {
  padding: 0.75rem;
  border-bottom: 0.1rem solid #E6E6E6;
}

#messages-modal li:hover {
  background-color: #E6E6E6;
}

#messages-modal li a:hover {
  text-decoration: none;
}

#messages-modal li img {
  max-width: 15%;
}
```

```
#messages-modal .msg-content {
  display: inline-block;
  color: #000;
}

#messages-modal .msg-content h5 {
  font-size: 1em;
  font-weight: bold;
}
```

In this CSS, we simply set a maximum height for the modal body, while adding a scroll overflow. For the list and the link, we changed the style for hover and adjusted the font weight, size, and color for display.

Refresh the web browser, click on the **Messages** link in the navigation bar and see your nice modal, as follows:

Summary

In this chapter, we finished our web application example. The main objective here was to learn about the Bootstrap plugins that we had not described before.

First, you learned about data attributes and how to use them with Bootstrap. After that, we saw both the possible ways to call plugins: via pure JavaScript or just through data attributes APIs.

We started and finished plugins with modals. Modals are one of the main plugins in Bootstrap because they are very versatile and customizable. Thus, they are fit for multiple contexts where you need some interaction with the user but do not want to move to another page.

In the middle of the chapter, we talked about two plugins that are closely related. They are the tooltip and the popover. Both came from the same initial plugin but with different contexts. Tooltips are used for auxiliary content, and popovers are something midway between a modal and a tooltip, so they can display more content compared to tooltips, but not too much intrusive like modals.

Creating a web application that is Twitter-like is an important kind of knowledge, since this can be replicated to different sources. Web applications have revolutionized the Web in different ways, and Bootstrap has taken the lead by helping us create faster and more beautiful web pages.

In the next chapter, we will step into an even more challenging example—we will build a dashboard web application from scratch! Just like the web application presented in this chapter, web dashboards are very popular across the Internet, and building one will place us at the same stratum as some of the best web developers. Ready for the advanced level?

Entering in the Advanced Mode

Alright, there is no more time to spend on testing our skills. Now it's time to truly test ourselves with a big challenge: creating an admin dashboard using Bootstrap. Now Bootstrap can help us, but we must know how to handle the majority of the framework to deliver professional work.

We need a plan to build this dashboard from scratch to its final form. Therefore, we will follow a designer template and recreate it from an image to a web page. Following this concept, you will learn about:

- The fluid container
- The flexbox layout
- Bootstrap custom stacked navigation
- The collapse plugin
- Bootstrap and advanced CSS
- External plugin integration
- Single-page application loading

This is the final example of the book. Let's face it and nail the Bootstrap framework. I know you are thoroughly able to defeat this final boss!

The master plan

As I mentioned, this is a professional job and it deserves a professional treatment. Now we will have a design guideline to follow. Up next is a screenshot of the dashboard that we have to reproduce by code:

As you can see, the dashboard is composed of a navigation header containing some information, a search bar, and notifications. On the left-hand side is a menu with the sections of the web application. In the center is a set of charts about the page status. It looks good in the screenshot and will look even better in the browser!

The page scaffolding consists of the following:

- The Bootstrap navigation component at the header, which is affixed to the top of the page
- A fluid container with two columns
- The left-hand-side column contains the dashboard menu and is affixed
- The right-hand-side column is the main content, which holds a set of cards that display some statistics

First of all, before you create any element, create a new file using the same structure that we pointed out for starting every example in the book (refer to the Bootstrap required tags section in *Chapter 1, Getting Started,* for more information). Create a file named `dashboard.html` and apply the default starter HTML to the file. Now we are ready to go!

The last navigation bar with flexbox

You may be bored of doing navigation bars; however, because of the acquired experience, we will do this one very quickly, taking advantage of the code written in previous examples.

Create a `<nav>` element, and inside it, create a `.container-fluid` and a `.row`:

```
<nav class="navbar navbar-fixed-top">
  <div class="container-fluid">
    <div class="row">
    </div>
  </div>
</nav>
```

This `.row` element will have two columns, just as we mentioned that will be done for the main container. On the first one, let's create the dashboard title and a refresh button, as follows:

```
<nav class="navbar navbar-fixed-top">
  <div class="container-fluid">
    <div class="row">
      <div class="col-sm-3 top-left-menu">
        <div class="navbar-header">
          <a class="navbar-brand" href="webapp.html">
            <h1>dashboard</h1>
          </a>
```

```
        </div>
        <a href="#" data-toggle="tooltip" data-placement="bottom"
data-delay="500" title="Refresh data" class="header-refresh pull-
right">
          <span class="glyphicon glyphicon-repeat" aria-
hidden="true"></span>
        </a>
      </div>
    </div>
  </div>
</nav>
```

Note that for the refresh button, we have used .glyphicon and added a tooltip. Do not forget to activate the tooltip in the main.js file that you have loaded:

```
$(document).ready(function() {
    $('[data-toggle="tooltip"]').tooltip();
});
```

In the tooltip, we added a delay to it show up with the data-delay="500" attribute. We mentioned this as an option for tooltip, but haven't made use of it so far. This will just delay the appearance of the tooltip for 500 milliseconds, while hovering the refresh link.

Inside .nav-header, add .navbar-toggle, which will be displayed for small screens and collapse the menu:

```
<nav class="navbar navbar-fixed-top">
  <div class="container-fluid">
    <div class="row">
      <div class="col-sm-3 top-left-menu">
        <div class="navbar-header">
          <a class="navbar-brand" href="webapp.html">
            <h1>dashboard</h1>
          </a>
          <button type="button" class="navbar-toggle collapsed"
data-toggle="collapse" data-target="#nav-menu" aria-expanded="false">
            <span class="sr-only">Toggle navigation</span>
            <span class="icon-bar"></span>
            <span class="icon-bar"></span>
            <span class="icon-bar"></span>
          </button>
        </div>
        <a href="#" data-toggle="tooltip" data-placement="bottom"
data-delay="500" title="Refresh data" class="header-refresh pull-
right">
```

```
            <span class="glyphicon glyphicon-repeat" aria-
hidden="true"></span>
          </a>
        </div>
      </div>
    </div>
</nav>
```

So far, we have no secrets. We have just replicated components that we used before. Following our pipeline, we should create some CSS rules to style our page, although first let's create some common CSS style. At the beginning of base.css, which is loaded in our HTML, we add the style:

```
.transition,
.transition:hover,
.transition:focus {

  -webkit-transition: all 150ms ease-in-out;
  -moz-transition: all 150ms ease-in-out;
  -ms-transition: all 150ms ease-in-out;
  -o-transition: all 150ms ease-in-out;
  transition: all 150ms ease-in-out;
}

html, body {
  position: relative;
  height: 100%;
  background-color: #e5e9ec;
}
```

First, we created a common .transition class to be used in multiples cases (we will use it in the chapter). Transitions were introduced in CSS3 and they allow us to create transition effects. In this case, it's an effect of ease-in-out for any element that has this class.

Also, for html and body, we changed the background and set the position and height to fill the entire screen.

Next, we must add the CSS for the navigation header:

```
nav.navbar-fixed-top {
  background-color: #FFF;
  border: none;
}
```

```css
nav .top-left-menu {
  background-color: #252830;
  display: -webkit-flex;
  display: flex;
  align-items: center;
}

.navbar-brand {
  height: auto;
}

.navbar-brand h1 {
  margin: 0;
  font-size: 1.5em;
  font-weight: 300;
  color: #FFF;
}

nav .header-refresh {
  margin-left: auto;
  color: #FFF;
}
```

Here, we changed the color of the elements. But the most important thing here is the usage of the `flexbox` rules (do you remember flexbox, which we discussed in *Chapter 5, Making It Fancy*, in the *Understanding flexbox* section?). Remember that Bootstrap 4 will support flex display, so it is nice to keep using it, since it should be the standard in the near future for every browser.

The result of this part must look like what is shown in the following screenshot:

The navigation search

Following our design, we have to create a search form. So, just after the closure of .top-left-menu, add the form code, such as the portion in bold:

```
<nav class="navbar navbar-fixed-top">
  <div class="container-fluid">
    <div class="row">
      <div class="col-sm-3 top-left-menu">
        ...
      </div>

      <form id="search" role="search" class="hidden-xs col-sm-3">
        <div class="input-group">
          <span class="glyphicon glyphicon-search" aria-
hidden="true"></span>
          <input type="text" class="form-control transition"
placeholder="Search...">
        </div>
      </form>

    </div>
  </div>
</nav>
```

As usual, it's CSS time:

```
nav form#search {
  padding: 0.9em;
}

nav form#search .input-group {
  display: -webkit-flex;
  display: flex;
  align-items: center;
}

nav form#search .input-group .form-control {
  border-radius: 0.25em;
  border: none;
  width: 70%;
```

```css
    padding-left: 1.9em;
    background-color: #F3F3F3;
    box-shadow: none;
}

nav form#search .input-group .form-control:focus {
    width: 100%;
    box-shadow: none;
}

nav form#search .glyphicon-search {
    z-index: 99;
    left: 1.7em;
}
```

In this CSS, we have again used the `display: flex` property. In addition to this, we created a pseudo-class rule for `.form-control`. The `:focus`, which is activated whenever the input has focus, in other words, is receiving some text. This `:focus` rule will change the width of the input when you focus the input, which happens when you click on it.

Refresh the web page and click on the input on the search form. Note that we applied the `.transition` class in this element, so when we focus it, the change of width is smoothed in a transition. The result should look like this:

The menu needs navigation

To finish the navigation bar, we have to create the right-hand-side content of the navigation bar, which we call #nav-menu. This menu will hold the notification list, placed as a button dropdown.

After <form>, place the presented HTML:

```html
<div id="nav-menu" class="collapse navbar-collapse pull-right">
  <ul class="nav navbar-nav">
  </ul>
</div>
```

Inside this `<ul>` tag, we will place the notifications. Right now, we just have this option, but with this list, we can add multiple items in the navigation bar. So, add the following code for the item:

```html
<div id="nav-menu" class="collapse navbar-collapse pull-right">
  <ul class="nav navbar-nav">
    <li>
      <div id="btn-notifications" class="btn-group">
        <span class="badge">3</span>
        <button type="button" class="btn btn-link dropdown-toggle"
data-toggle="dropdown" aria-haspopup="true" aria-expanded="false">
          Notifications
        </button>
      </div>
    </li>
  </ul>
</div>
```

Explaining this item, we can say that it is a button for the notification. There is a wrapper element named `#btn-notifications`. Inside it is a `.badge` to verbalize the number of new notifications, and a `button.btn` that must seem like a link, so we applied the `.btn-link` class to it. The button also contains the tags needed for a Bootstrap drop-down button, such as the `.dropdown-toggle` class and the `data-toggle="dropdown"` data property.

Therefore, every `button.dropdown-toggle` button needs a `ul.dropdown-menu`. Just after `<button>`, create the list:

```html
<div id="nav-menu" class="collapse navbar-collapse pull-right">
  <ul class="nav navbar-nav">
    <li>
      <div id="btn-notifications" class="btn-group">
        <span class="badge">3</span>
        <button type="button" class="btn btn-link dropdown-toggle"
data-toggle="dropdown" aria-haspopup="true" aria-expanded="false">
          Notifications
        </button>
        <ul id="notification-list" class="dropdown-menu pull-right">
          <li>
            <a href="#">
              <span class="badge"></span>
              <img src="imgs/laika.jpg" class="img-circle">
              <div class="notification-message">
                <strong>Laika</strong>
                <p>Hey! How are you?</p>
```

```
            <em class="since">2h ago</em>
          </div>
        </a>
      </li>
      <li>
        <a href="#">
          <span class="badge"></span>
          <img src="imgs/cat.jpg" class="img-circle">
          <div class="notification-message">
            <strong>Devil cat</strong>
            <p>I will never forgive you...</p>
            <em class="since">6h ago</em>
          </div>
        </a>
      </li>
      <li>
        <a href="#">
          <span class="badge"></span>
          <img src="imgs/doge.jpg" class="img-circle">
          <div class="notification-message">
            <strong>Doge</strong>
            <p>What are you doing? So scare. It's alright
now.</p>
            <em class="since">yesterday</em>
          </div>
        </a>
      </li>
    </ul>
  </div>
</li>
</ul>
</div>
```

The new list element is pointed out in bold. Even though the content seems long, it is just a repetition of three items with different contents inside our notification list.

Refresh the page, open the dropdown, and you will feel an uncontrollable desire to add some CSS and stop the dropdown from being ugly anymore:

```
/*nav menu*/
nav #nav-menu {
  padding: 0.4em;
  padding-right: 1em;
}
```

```
/*nav menu and notifications*/
#nav-menu #btn-notifications > .badge {
  color: #FFF;
  background-color: #f35958;
  font-size: 0.7em;
  padding: 0.3rem 0.55rem 0.3rem 0.5rem;
  position: absolute;
  right: -0.4rem;
  top: 1rem;
  z-index: 99;
}

#btn-notifications .btn-link {
  padding-top: 1.5rem;
  color: #252830;
  font-weight: 500;
}

#btn-notifications .btn-link:hover {
  text-decoration: none;
}
```

Great! This will make the button and notification badge appear more beautiful. Then it's time for `#notification-list`:

```
#notification-list {
  max-height: 20em;
  overflow: auto;
}

#notification-list a {
  display: -webkit-flex;
  display: flex;
  opacity: 0.7;
  margin: 1.5rem;
  border-radius: 0.5rem;
  padding: 0.5rem 1.3rem;
  background-color: #EFEFEF;
  position: relative;
}

#notification-list a:hover {
  color: #262626;
  text-decoration: none;
  opacity: 1;
```

```
}

#notification-list img {
  display: inline-block;
  height: 35px;
  width: 35px;
  margin-right: 1em;
  margin-top: 1em;
}

#notification-list .notification-message {
  display: inline-block;
  white-space: normal;
  min-width: 25rem;
}

#notification-list .badge:empty {
  display: inline-block;
  position: absolute;
  right: 0.5rem;
  top: 0.5rem;
  background-color: #f35958;
  height: 1.4rem;
}

#notification-list em.since {
  font-size: 0.7em;
  color: #646C82;
}
```

For the notification, we did just some common rules, such as spacing, color, and so on. The only different thing is, again, the use of `flexbox` to align the content. See this screenshot for the final result of the navigation bar:

 Did you notice that the images appear rounded? Do you know why? This is because of the `.img-circle` Bootstrap helper class; it is present in every `<img>` element.

Checking the profile

In the navigation bar, the last present component is a picture that, when you click on it, opens a user menu, just like what we did in the example of the web application. With no further delay, place the next HTML just after the `<ul>` of #nav-menu:

```html
<div id="nav-menu" class="collapse navbar-collapse pull-right">
  <ul class="nav navbar-nav">

    ...

  </ul>


  <div id="nav-profile" class="btn-group pull-right">
    <button type="button" class="btn btn-link dropdown-toggle
thumbnail" data-toggle="dropdown" aria-haspopup="true" aria-
expanded="false">
      <img src="imgs/jon.png" class="img-circle">
    </button>
    <ul class="dropdown-menu">
      <li><a href="#">Profile</a></li>
      <li><a href="settings.html">Setting</a></li>
      <li role="separator" class="divider"></li>
      <li><a href="#">Logout</a></li>
    </ul>
  </div>
</div>
```

So, it is another button dropdown. The CSS for this HTML is as follows:

```css
#nav-profile {
  margin: 0.5em;
  margin-left: 1em;
}

#nav-profile button.thumbnail {
  margin: 0;
  padding: 0;
  border: 0;
}

#nav-profile img {
  max-height: 2.3em;
}
```

We are done! Refresh the web browser and see the result, which should be like what is shown in this screenshot:

Filling the main fluid content

After the navigation bar, we must fill the main content using a fluid layout. For that, we create a `.container-fluid`, just as we did in the `<nav>`. Inside the container, we create a single `.row` and two columns with spacing three and nine, respectively:

```
<div class="container-fluid">
  <div class="row">
    <div id="side-menu" class="col-md-3 hidden-xs">
    </div>

    <div id="main" class="col-md-9">
    </div>
  </div>
</div>
```

It is a common grid, containing one row. In the row, the first column, `#side-menu`, is shown from small viewports up to larger ones, while the `#main` column fills 9 out of 12 grids for medium resolutions.

However, we must not forget that `#side-menu` is actually an affix component. So, let's add the data properties to make it stitch to the top of the page, as we did in the web application example when you were learning this plugin:

```
<div class="container-fluid">
  <div class="row">
    <div id="side-menu" class="col-md-3 hidden-xs" data-spy="affix"
data-offset-top="0">
    </div>

    <div id="main" class="col-sm-offset-3 col-md-9">
    </div>
```

```
    </div>
  </div>
```

Note that because of the addition of the affix, we must set an offset in the `#main` div with the `.col-sm-offset-3` class.

From the side stacked menu

Let's fill `#side-menu` with content. At first, we have to create the profile block, which contains the user data. Place the following HTML inside the referred element:

```html
<div id="side-menu" class="col-md-3 hidden-xs" data-spy="affix"
data-offset-top="0">
  <div class="profile-block">
    <img src="imgs/jon.png" class="img-circle">
    <h4 class="profile-title">Jonny Doo
<small>@jonnydoo</small></h4>
  </div>
</div>
```

Check out the page in the browser, and you will see that it is not displaying nicely. For the CSS, we must follow this style:

```css
#side-menu {
  background-color: #1b1e24;
  padding-top: 7.2rem;
  height: 100%;
  position: fixed;
}

#side-menu .profile-block > * {
  display: inline-block;
}

#side-menu .profile-block img {
  width: 70px;
}

#side-menu .profile-title {
  color: #FFF;
  margin-left: 1rem;
  font-size: 1.5em;
  vertical-align: middle;
}

#side-menu .profile-title small {
  display: block;
}
```

With that, the #side-menu should fill the entire left height, but if you resize the browser to a smaller resolution, you will see that #nav-header does not resize together with the main content. This is a small challenge. Do you know why it is happening?

That was a little prank! Did I get you? In #side-menu, we applied only the class for medium viewports, that is, the .col-md-3 class. What we should have done was apply the class for small devices as well to make it responsive to small viewports and resize like all the other elements, which needs the .col-sm-* class. In this case, just change the class of #side-menu and in the #main element as well:

```
<div class="container-fluid">
  <div class="row">
     <div id="side-menu" class="col-sm-3 hidden-xs" data-spy="affix"
data-offset-top="0">
     </div>

     <div id="main" class="col-sm-offset-3 col-sm-9">
     </div>
  </div>
</div>
```

Here is a screenshot that shows the result of the side menu for the moment:

I heard that the left menu is great!

A web application is never a web application if it does not have a menu. After the profile info in #side-menu, we will add a stacked menu.

Hearing the word "stacked" for a menu, what you remember? Of course, the .nav-stacked menu from Bootstrap! Let's create a .nav-stacked component in this menu. Therefore, after #profile-block, append the following HTML:

```
<ul class="nav nav-pills nav-stacked">
   <li>
```

```html
      <a href="#" class="transition">
        <span class="glyphicon glyphicon-home" aria-hidden="true"></
span>
        Overview
      </a>
    </li>
    <li>
      <a href="#" class="transition">
        <span class="glyphicon glyphicon-user" aria-hidden="true"></
span>
        Audience
      </a>
    </li>
    <li>
      <a href="#" class="transition">
        <span class="glyphicon glyphicon-usd" aria-hidden="true"></span>
        Finances
        <span class="glyphicon glyphicon-menu-left pull-right
transition" aria-hidden="true"></span>
      </a>
    </li>
    <li>
      <a href="#" class="transition">
        <span class="glyphicon glyphicon-time" aria-hidden="true"></
span>
        Real time
        <span class="badge pull-right">12</span>
      </a>
    </li>
    <li class="nav-divider"></li>
    <li>
      <a href="#" class="transition">
        <span class="glyphicon glyphicon-briefcase" aria-
hidden="true"></span>
        Projects
        <span class="glyphicon glyphicon-menu-left pull-right
transition" aria-hidden="true"></span>
      </a>
    </li>
  </ul>
```

No secrets here! Just create a simple stacked list using the .nav, .nav-pills, and .nav-stacked classes. Bootstrap will do the magic for you. You will learn a little trick now—the collapse Bootstrap plugin.

Learning the collapse plugin

Collapse is another plugin from Bootstrap that toggles the visualization behavior of an element. It will show or collapse an item regarding the trigger of an action.

 The collapse plugin requires the transition plugin present in the Bootstrap framework.

To add the collapse event to an element, you should add a data attribute called `data-toggle="collapse"`. If the element is a link `<a>`, point the anchor to the identifier of the element, like this: `href="#my-collapsed-element"`. If it is a `<button>`, add the data attribute pointing the identifier, like this for instance: `data-target="#my-collapsed-element"`. The difference between using `href` for a link and `data-target` for a `button` is because of the semantics of the element. Naturally, every link is expected to have a reference in the `href`, although we do not have this requirement in buttons. So, Bootstrap binds the element through a `data-target` data attribute.

We will create a sublist in our menu using the collapse plugin for the **Finances** and **Projects** entries. After the link of each one of these items, create a secondary list, as is pointed in the following highlighted HTML. Also, since we are using `<a>` tags, we add to the `href` the identifier of the element that will be collapsed and the `data-toggle` corresponding to collapse:

```html
<ul class="nav nav-pills nav-stacked">
  <li>
    <a href="#" class="transition">
      <span class="glyphicon glyphicon-home" aria-hidden="true"></span>
      Overview
    </a>
  </li>
  <li>
    <a href="#" class="transition">
      <span class="glyphicon glyphicon-user" aria-hidden="true"></span>
      Audience
    </a>
  </li>
  <li>
    <a href="#finances-opts" class="transition" role="button" data-toggle="collapse" aria-expanded="false" aria-controls="finances-opts">
```

```
      <span class="glyphicon glyphicon-usd" aria-hidden="true"></span>
      Finances
      <span class="glyphicon glyphicon-menu-left pull-right
transition" aria-hidden="true"></span>
  </a>
  <ul class="collapse list-unstyled" id="finances-opts">
    <li>
      <a href="#" class="transition">
        Incomes
      </a>
    </li>
    <li>
      <a href="#" class="transition">
        Outcomes
      </a>
    </li>
  </ul>
</li>
<li>
  <a href="#" class="transition">
    <span class="glyphicon glyphicon-time" aria-hidden="true"></
span>
    Real time
    <span class="badge pull-right">12</span>
  </a>
</li>
<li class="nav-divider"></li>
<li>
  <a href="#projects-opts" class="transition" role="button"
data-toggle="collapse" aria-expanded="false" aria-controls="projects-
opts">
    <span class="glyphicon glyphicon-briefcase" aria-
hidden="true"></span>
    Projects
    <span class="glyphicon glyphicon-menu-left pull-right
transition" aria-hidden="true"></span>
  </a>
  <ul class="collapse list-unstyled" id="projects-opts">
    <li>
      <a href="#" class="transition">
        Free ration nation
      </a>
    </li>
    <li>
```

```
        <a href="#" class="transition">
          Cats going crazy
        </a>
      </li>
    </ul>
  </li>
</ul>
```

To make it clear, take as an example the first collapsed menu from **Finances**. Below the **Finances** link, we created the list to be collapsed, identified by `#finances-opt`. We also added the `.collapse` class, which is a Bootstrap class used to collapse elements.

Going back to the **Finances** link, add to the `href` the ID of the collapsed list, `#finances-opt`. Also, we added the `data-toggle="collapse"` required to Bootstrap Collapse work. Finally, we added the aria attributes, `aria-controls` and `aria-controls`, for semantic notation.

Refresh the browser and you will see how Bootstrap does almost the entire job for us. In the CSS, we need to add some simple styles for color and spacing:

```css
#side-menu ul.nav {
  margin-top: 1rem;
}

#side-menu ul.nav a {
  color: #8b91a0;
}

#side-menu ul.nav a:hover,
#side-menu ul.nav a:focus {
  color: #FFF;
  background-color: inherit;
}

#side-menu ul.nav a .glyphicon {
  margin-right: 0.7rem;
}

#side-menu ul.nav a .glyphicon.pull-right {
  margin-top: 0.2rem;
}

#side-menu ul.nav a .badge {
  background-color: #1ca095;
```

```
}

#side-menu ul.nav .nav-divider {
  background-color: #252830;
}

#side-menu ul.nav ul {
  margin-left: 10%;
}

#side-menu ul.nav ul a {
  display: block;
  background-color: #2b303b;
  padding: 1rem;
  margin-bottom: 0.3rem;
  border-radius: 0.25em;
}

#side-menu ul.nav ul a:hover {
  text-decoration: none;
  background-color: #434857;
}
```

Go to the browser and refresh it to see the result. It should look like what is shown in this screenshot:

Using some advanced CSS

Let's add a cherry to this pie while learning other CSS properties. What do you think if we could rotate the arrow of the items that have collapsed menus by 90 degrees anticlockwise to create an opening effect? It would be awesome—even more if we did that with only CSS.

Add the next CSS rule for the effect using the `transform` property:

```
#side-menu ul.nav a:focus .glyphicon.pull-right {
  -moz-transform: rotate(-90deg);
  -webkit-transform: rotate(-90deg);
  -o-transform: rotate(-90deg);
  -ms-transform: rotate(-90deg);
  transform: rotate(-90deg);
}
```

This `transform` property will do exactly what we want; when the link is in focus (which means it is clicked on), the icon from the arrow will rotate 90 degrees anticlockwise, because of the minus signal.

To be more pro, let's use a supernew property called `will-change`. Add the style to the following selector:

```
#side-menu ul.nav a .glyphicon.pull-right {
  margin-top: 0.2rem;
  will-change: transform;
}
```

The will-change property

The `will-change` property optimizes animations by letting the browser know which elements will change and need careful treatment. Currently, this property is not supported by all browsers, but soon it will be. Check out its availability at `http://caniuse.com/#feat=will-change`.

Click to open a submenu and see the opening menu animation with the arrow rotation. The next screenshot presents an open menu:

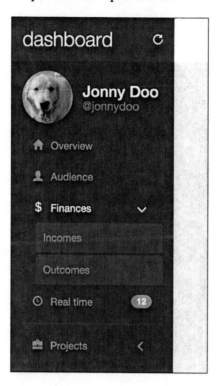

Filling the main content

To finish the content of the first step of our dashboard, we will move on to the main content, referred to by the column identified by `#main`. In this section, we will create a set of cards almost similar to the cards made in the web application demo, along with the use of some external plugins for chart generation.

However, before everything else, we need to create some common CSS in our main content. Add the following style to the base.css file:

```css
#main {
  padding-top: 7.2rem;
  display: -webkit-flex;
  display: flex;
  align-items: stretch;
  flex-flow: row wrap;
}

.card {
  position: relative;
  border-radius: 0.25em;
  box-shadow: 0 1px 4px 0 rgba(0, 0, 0, 0.37);
  background-color: #FFF;
  margin: 1.25rem;
  flex-grow: 5;
}

.card * {
  color: #252830;
}

.card-block {
  padding: 2rem;
}

.card-block h2 {
  margin: 0;
  margin-bottom: 1.5rem;
  color: #252830;
}
```

As I said, we will play with cards inside this element, so let's create the classes that relate to it almost similarly to what we did in the cards for the web application example. In this case, even though you are using Bootstrap 4, you must add to those classes to correctly style the cards component.

Our first card will be placed inside the `#main` element. So, create the following HTML. The first card will be an **Overall analysis** card:

```html
<div id="main" class="col-sm-offset-3 col-sm-9">
  <div class="card" id="pie-charts">
    <div class="card-block">
      <h2>Overall analysis</h2>


    </div>
  </div>
</div>
```

Rounding the charts

The first plugin that we will use is called *Easy Pie Chart* (`https://rendro.github.io/easy-pie-chart/`). This plugin generates only rounded pie charts. It is a lightweight, single-purpose plugin.

In order to use this plugin, you can get it through bower, through npm, or by simply downloading the ZIP file from the repository. In any case, what you will need to do at the end is load the plugin in the HTML file.

We will use the jQuery version of the plugin, so we place the JavaScript file in our `js` folder and load the plugin at the end of our file:

```html
<script src="js/jquery-1.11.3.js"></script>
<script src="js/bootstrap.js"></script>
<script src="js/jquery.easypiechart.min.js"></script>
<script src="js/main.js"></script>
```

Inside our `#pie-charts` card that we just created, let's add some HTML that is needed for the corresponding plugin:

```html
<div class="card" id="pie-charts">
  <div class="card-block">
    <h2>Overall analysis</h2>
    <div class="round-chart" data-percent="42">
      <span>
        42
        <small>
          % <br>
          recurring
        </small>
      </span>
    </div>
```

```
<div class="round-chart" data-percent="87">
  <span>
    87
    <small>
      % <br>
      aware
    </small>
  </span>
</div>
</div>
</div>
```

To make the *Easy Pie Chart* plugin work, you must apply it to an element, and you can pass arguments by data attributes. For example, in this case, we have `data-percent`, which will say the fill of the chart.

Go to your JavaScript file (the `main.js` file), and inside the `ready` function (just as we did in *Chapter 8, Working with JavaScript, Creating our custom modal*), add the following code to initialize the plugin:

```
$(document).ready(function() {
    $('.round-chart').easyPieChart({
        'scaleColor': false,
        'lineWidth': 20,
        'lineCap': 'butt',
        'barColor': '#6d5cae',
        'trackColor': '#e5e9ec',
        'size': 190
    });
});
```

What we are telling here is the style of the chart. But we need more style! We append the following CSS to our `base.css`:

```
.round-chart {
  display: inline-block;
  position: relative;
}

.round-chart + .round-chart {
  float: right;
}

.round-chart span {
  font-size: 3em;
```

```
    font-weight: 100;
    line-height: 1.7rem;
    width: 12rem;
    height: 4.4rem;
    text-align: center;
    position: absolute;
    margin: auto;
    top: 0;
    bottom: 0;
    left: 0;
    right: 0;
}

.round-chart span > small {
    font-size: 2rem;
    font-weight: 400;
}
```

What we are doing here, besides changing some spacing, is the centralization of the percentage text that we have added. Refresh the page and you should see something like this:

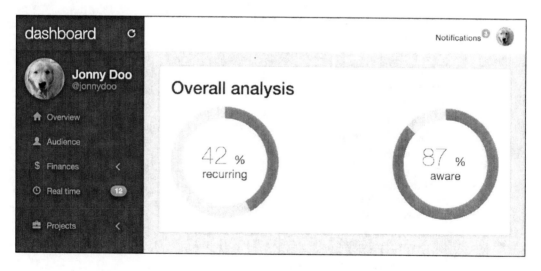

As you can see, the card has filled the entire line. This is because of the `flexbox` layout that we are using in the `#main` element. Check out the CSS that we used for this element:

```
#main {
    padding-top: 7.2rem;
```

```
    display: -webkit-flex;
    display: flex;
    align-items: stretch;
    flex-flow: row wrap;
}
```

With the `flex` display, if we use `align-items: stretch`, the layout will stretch to fill the content in the cross axis.

The `flex-flow` style is a shorthand for `flex-direction` and `flex-wrap`. By using this property, we can apply both options to specify the direction of the items, in this case as a `row`, and set the row to wrap to the next lines.

Also, for each card, we have created the `flex-grow: 5` property, which says to the element that it can assume five different sizes inside the `#main` container.

Creating a quick statistical card

The next card contains statistical information and we will create it just by using Bootstrap components. So, after the `#pie-charts` card, create another one in HTML:

```html
<div class="card" id="quick-info">
  <div class="card-block">
    <h2>Quick stats</h2>
    <div class="quick-stats">
      <strong>Today:</strong>
      <span>78</span>
    </div>
    <div class="quick-stats">
      <strong>This month:</strong>
      <span>459</span>
    </div>
    <div class="quick-stats">
      <strong>All time:</strong>
      <span>54k</span>
    </div>
    <div class="quick-stats">
      <strong>Bounce rate:</strong>
      <span>81.08%</span>
    </div>
```

```
    <div class="quick-stats">
      <strong>Session duration:</strong>
      <span>00:01:41</span>
    </div>
    <div class="quick-stats">
      <strong>New session:</strong>
      <span>63.86%</span>
    </div>
  </div>
</div>
```

The #quick-info card contains only the common elements that will be displayed, each one in a line inside .card. Add the next CSS style to correctly display this card:

```
#quick-info .card-block {
  display: flex;
  flex-direction: column;
}

#quick-info .quick-stats {
  font-size: 2rem;
  line-height: 3rem;
  border-bottom: 0.1rem solid #e5e9ec;
}

#quick-info .quick-stats strong {
  font-weight: 300;
}

#quick-info .quick-stats span {
  font-weight: 300;
  float: right;
  color: #8b91a0;
}
```

In the web browser, you should see the following result:

But wait! If you look at the initial layout, you will realize that those two cards should be displayed side by side! What happened here?

This is another advantage of using the flexbox! With a flex display, each item inside the container will adapt for the display. The previous screenshot was taken from a medium viewport. If you take it from a large-resolution screen, you will see how the elements appear side by side, like this:

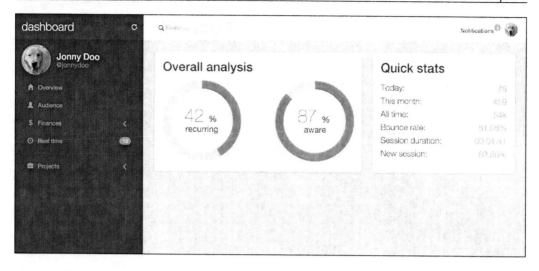

Getting a spider chart

The next chart is called a spider chart. The Highcharts plugin (`http://www.highcharts.com/`) is one of the most definitive plugins used to create charts. It provides a wide variety of charts divided over different modules, so you can load only the plugins that you will use.

Just like Easy Pie Chart, you can get Highcharts from different sources. After getting it, let's load the first Highcharts module that we need. Load them along with the other JavaScript files (the plugin is loaded using CDN in this case):

```
<script src="https://code.highcharts.com/highcharts.js"></script>
<script src="https://code.highcharts.com/highcharts-more.js"></script>
```

Create another `.card` in the HTML after `#quick-info`, this new one being identified by `#performance-eval`:

```
<div class="card" id="performance-eval">
  <div class="card-block">
    <h2>Performance evaluation</h2>
    <div class="spider-chart"></div>
  </div>
</div>
```

Highcharts does not require too much HTML, but you need to customize it all over JavaScript. To initialize and customize the plugin, add the following code inside the ready function of the JavaScript:

```javascript
$('#performance-eval .spider-chart').highcharts({

    chart: {
        polar: true,
        type: 'area'
    },

    title: {
        text: ''
    },

    xAxis: {
        categories: ['Taming', 'Acessory', 'Development',
'Grooming', 'Awareness', 'Ration'],
        tickmarkPlacement: 'on',
        lineWidth: 0
    },

    yAxis: {
        gridLineInterpolation: 'polygon',
        lineWidth: 0,
        min: 0
    },

    tooltip: {
        shared: true,
        pointFormat: '<span style="color:{series.color}">{series.
name}:
<b>${point.y:,.0f}</b><br/>' --
    },

    legend: {
        align: 'right',
        verticalAlign: 'top',
        y: 70,
        layout: 'vertical'
    },

    series: [{
        name: 'Allocated resources',
```

```
            data: [45000, 39000, 58000, 63000, 38000, 93000],
            pointPlacement: 'on',
            color: '#676F84'
        },
        {

            name: 'Spent resources',
            data: [83000, 49000, 60000, 35000, 77000, 90000],
            pointPlacement: 'on',
            color: '#f35958'
        }]


    });
```

In this JavaScript code, we called the `highcharts` function for the selector chart `#performance-eval .spider-chart`. All the properties are fully described in the official documentation. Just note that we instructed the chart that we want a polar chart with the `polar: true` key inside the `chart` key option.

The dashboard application must look and feel like this:

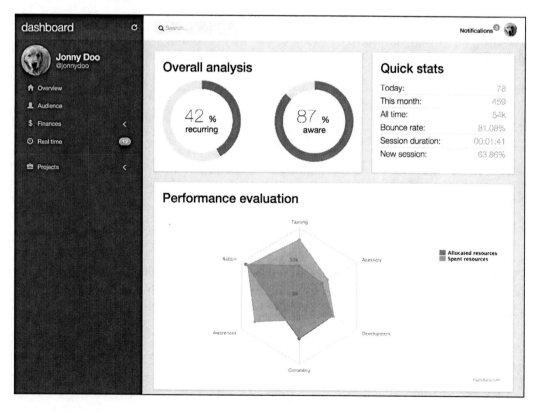

Overhead loading

Another cool feature from these plugins is that they provide animations for charts, making the final result very user friendly.

By loading the pieces of JavaScript code at the end of the HTML, we will acquire more speed in page rendering for the end user. The side effect of this is that the elements created by the JavaScript libraries will render the page after it is shown to the user, causing some temporary glitches in the screen.

To solve this, many pages use the strategy of creating an overlay loading that will be hidden after the document is ready.

To do this, just after the opening of the `<body>` tag, create a `<div>` to keep the loading, as follows:

```
<body>
  <div class="loading">
  </div>
  … <!--rest of the HTML content -->
</body>
```

We added a loading animated `.svg` file in the images folder, so in the CSS, we create the following rules:

```
.loading {
  position: fixed;
  z-index: 999;
  width: 100%;
  height: 100%;
  background-image: url('../imgs/loading.svg');
  background-repeat: no-repeat;
  background-attachment: fixed;
  background-position: center;
  background-color: #e5e9ec;
}
```

This will create an overlay element that will appear at the top of all elements, except for the navigation bar. This element will fill the complete width and height of the page, while containing the loading animated image in the center of it.

Refresh the page and you will see the loading on top of your dashboard web application, as follows:

Now we must remove the loading image after the page is ready. So, in the beginning of the JavaScript file, before the first line inside the $(document).ready function, remove the loading element:

```
$(document).ready(function() {
    // when page is loaded, remove the loading
    $('.loading').remove();
    // below goes the rest of the JavaScript code
});
```

Done! Refresh the web browser and you may see the loading screen depending on your computer and network.

The loading element may see an overreaction now, because we still do not have too many cards on our dashboard, but we will keep adding them, so it is cautious to start handling this problem.

Fixing the toggle button for mobile

We created our page using the principles of mobile-first development, although some of the components here are not appearing properly or are simply not appearing, and we must fix that.

First is the toggle button, `.navbar-toggle`, in the navigation bar. It is actually appearing, but with a really bad colorization. Let's fix that with some CSS:

```css
.navbar-toggle {
  border-color: #252830;
  background-color: #e5e9ec;
  margin-top: 13px
}

.navbar-toggle .icon-bar {
  background-color: #252830;
}
```

The toggle button should appear like what is shown in the next screenshot, now using gray colors:

As you can see, there are many other things that we can do to improve the visualization in mobiles and small viewports. We will fix all that in the next chapters while adding some more cool effects. Wait and you will see!

Summary

In this chapter, we started another example — the dashboard web application.

At first, it may appear a little difficult, but we are breaking down every line of code to explain it while using the top of the methodologies for frontend development.

This time, we have an initial design that we aim to create. This is cool because we do have a guideline on what we must do towards our final goal. Usually, when working in a project, you have this kind of scenario.

First, we created another navigation bar, this one being a little more complicated, using a fluid container. The rest of the navigation was made using almost the same methodology that we used when learning about this Bootstrap component.

On the left-hand-side menu, we customized the Bootstrap stacked navigation component, and you learned how to use the Bootstrap collapse plugin.

In the main content, we started to import external plugins to create nice charts for our dashboard. Also, we used the flex display to increase responsiveness, while using the best of CSS.

Finally, we created a loading element and fixed the first issue regarding viewports. Let's continue fixing this in the upcoming chapters.

Congratulations! The first chapter of the final example is nailed! I am pretty sure that you were able to understand the development concepts and how Bootstrap greatly increases our productivity.

In the next chapter, we will continue the construction of the dashboard — moreover, the main content — adding more external plugins and cards using Bootstrap components. We will also fix known issues for different viewports and explain the remaining Bootstrap plugins.

10
Bringing Components to Life

The last chapter was tough! Although the dashboard is not ready yet, following our layout, we must create three more cards in the main, while fixing issues regarding visualization for multiple viewports. After that, we will move on to creating more components for our dashboard. Let's proceed towards this new challenge!

In this chapter, we will cover the following topics:

- A custom checkbox
- External plugin integration
- Advanced Bootstrap media queries
- The viewport's advanced adjustments
- The Bootstrap Carousel plugin
- The Bootstrap Scrollspy plugin

Creating the main cards

Taking a look at our layout, we must create three more cards. The first of them is the hardest one, so let's face it!

The following .card is composed of an area chart with two series and some iOS-styled checkboxes. This screenshot reminds us of what the card must look like:

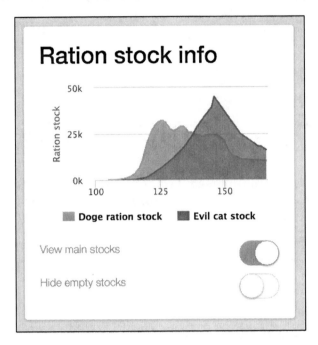

For the chart area, we will again use the highcharts library, while for the checkbox, we will use a plugin called switchery (https://github.com/abpetkov/switchery). After we've considered the documentation, let's create the following HTML:

```
<div class="card" id="ration-stock">
  <div class="card-block">
    <h2>Ration stock info</h2>
    <div class="stacked-area"></div>
    <div class="switch">
      View main stocks
      <input type="checkbox" class="swithcery" checked />
      <div class="clearfix"></div>
    </div>
    <div class="switch">
      Hide empty stocks
      <input type="checkbox" class="swithcery" />
      <div class="clearfix"></div>
    </div>
  </div>
</div>
```

Breaking the code down, to create the chart, we just have to set the `div.stacked-area` element. For the checkbox, we must create an input with `type="checkbox"` and the `.switchery` class to identify it.

Load the CSS of switchery in `<head>`, after the Bootstrap CSS:

```
<link rel="stylesheet" href="css/switchery.min.css">
```

Also, in the HTML, import the `switchery` library in the bottom part that contains the JavaScript loads:

```
<script src="js/switchery.min.js"></script>
```

We do not need much CSS here, since most of it will be created by JavaScript. So, just add the following rules to specify the height of the chart and the font style for the checkbox text:

```
#ration-stock .stacked-area {
  height: 200px;
}

#ration-stock .switch {
  font-weight: 300;
  color: #8b91a0;
  padding: 0.5rem 0;
}

#ration-stock .switchery {
  float: right;
}
```

The JavaScript contains the core portion of this card. First, let's initialize the switchery plugin. In `main.js`, inside the `.ready` function, add these lines:

```
var elems, switcheryOpts;

elems =
Array.prototype.slice.call(document.querySelectorAll('.switchery'));

switcheryOpts = {
    color: '#1bc98e'
};

elems.forEach(function(el) {
    var switchery = new Switchery(el, switcheryOpts);
});
```

In `elems`, we store the elements that contain the `.switchery` class. This plugin does not use jQuery, so we must create a query using native JavaScript. The query needed to select the elements follows the one provided in the documentation, and I recommend that you check it out for further information, since this is not the main focus of the book.

The query is performed by `document.querySelectorAll('.switchery')`. `Array` is a global JavaScript object used to create high-level list objects present in most recent browsers.

 The prototype is an object present on every JavaScript object. It contains a set of properties and methods for the regarding object.

The `slice` function chops the array using a shallow copy into another array. In summary, we are getting an array of elements with the `.switchery` class.

Next, we set the options for the plugin, in this case just the background color, using the `color` property in the `switcheryOpts` variable. Finally, we start each `Switchery` object inside the `forEach` loop.

Refresh the web page and the new card should appear as what is shown in the following screenshot:

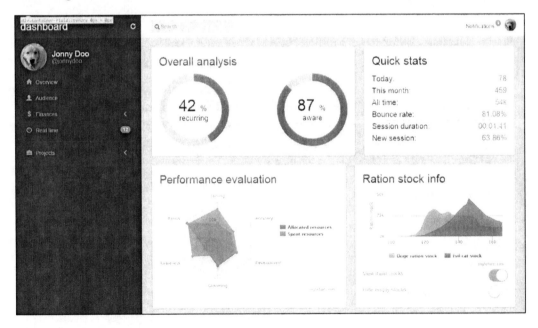

The other card using Bootstrap components

To create the next card, we will use the Bootstrap progress bar component, labels, and badges. This card represents some kind of real-time information, and we will create it using the progress bar and make it animated through JavaScript.

First, let's create this new card identified by `#real-time` in the HTML. Place the code after the last card, `#ration-stock`:

```
<div class="card" id="real-time">
  <div class="card-block">
  <h2>Real time information</h2>
  </div>
</div>
```

After `<h2>`, we must create a list containing each item of the information. A label, a badge, a progress bar, and a piece of sample text compose the list. Create it like the highlighted HTML code shown here:

```
<div class="card" id="real-time">
  <div class="card-block">
  <h2>Real time information</h2>
    <ul class="list-unstyled">
      <li>
        Active dogs:
        <span class="label label-warning pull-right">255</span>
      </li>
      <li>
        Silo status:
        <span class="badge ok pull-right">
          <span class="glyphicon glyphicon-ok" aria-hidden="true"></span>
        </span>
      </li>
      <li>
        Usage level:
        <div class="progress">
          <div class="progress-bar progress-bar-success" role="progressbar" aria-valuenow="25" aria-valuemin="0" aria-valuemax="100" style="width: 25%">
            <span class="sr-only">25%</span>
          </div>
          <div class="progress-bar progress-bar-warning progress-bar-striped active" role="progressbar" aria-valuenow="38" aria-valuemin="0" aria-valuemax="100" style="width: 38%">
```

```
            <span class="sr-only">38% alocated</span>
          </div>
          <div class="progress-bar progress-bar-danger"
  role="progressbar" aria-valuenow="5" aria-valuemin="0" aria-
  valuemax="100" style="width: 5%">
            <span class="sr-only">5% reserved</span>
          </div>
        </div>
      </li>
      <li>
        Free space:
        <span id="free-space" class="pull-right">
          32%
        </span>
      </li>
    </ul>
  </div>
</div>
```

Because we are mostly using only Bootstrap elements and components, we do not need too much CSS but just the following:

```
#real-time li {
  font-size: 1.8rem;
  font-weight: 300;
  border-bottom: 0.1rem solid #e5e9ec;
  padding: 0.5rem 0;
}

#real-time .badge.ok {
  background-color: #1bc98e;
}

#real-time .badge span,
#real-time .label {
  color: #FFF;
}

#real-time .badge,
#real-time .label {
  margin-top: 0.25rem;
}
```

This CSS will change the font size of the text in the card and the borders from one to another item in the list. Also, for the badge and the labels, we've customized the colors and margins.

Refresh the page and it should look like this:

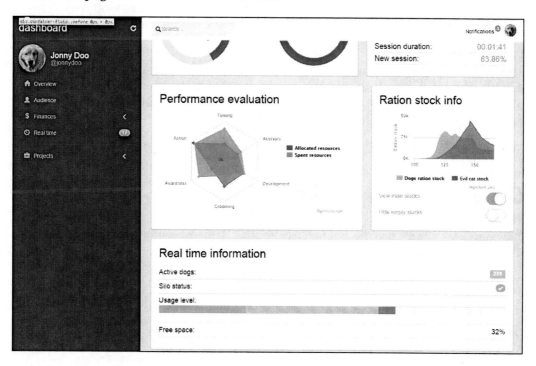

The new card looks nice! Now let's create some CSS to animate it. Let's change the free space percentage periodically. To do this, create the following JavaScript function:

```
changeMultiplier = 0.2;
window.setInterval(function() {
  var freeSpacePercentage;

  freeSpacePercentage = $('#free-space').text();
  freeSpacePercentage = parseFloat(freeSpacePercentage);

  delta = changeMultiplier * (Math.random() < 0.5 ? -1.0 : 1.0);

  freeSpacePercentage = freeSpacePercentage + freeSpacePercentage
* delta;
  freeSpacePercentage = parseInt(freeSpacePercentage);

  $('#free-space').text(freeSpacePercentage + '%');
}, 2000);
```

With this JavaScript code, we are executing a function every 2 seconds. We did this because of the usage of the `setInterval` function, and we call it every 2,000 ms (or 2 seconds).

What is done first is just a parse of the text inside the `#free-space` percentage element. Then we create a delta that could be 20 percent positive or negative, randomly generated by using the `changeMultiplier` parameter.

Finally, we multiply the delta by the current value and update the value in the element. To update the value in the element, we use the `.text()` function from jQuery. This function sets the content for the element to the specified text passed as a parameter; in this case, it's the percentage change in `freeSpacePercentage` that we randomly generated.

Refresh the page and see the number update every 2 seconds.

Creating our last plot

The last card in the main content is another plot, this time a pie chart. Just like the last charts, let's again use the Highcharts library. Remember that we must first create a simple HTML card, placed after the last `#real-time` card:

```
<div class="card" id="daily-usage">
  <div class="card-block">
    <h2>Daily usage</h2>
    <div class="area-chart"></div>
  </div>
</div>
```

In the CSS, just set the height of the plot:

```
#daily-usage .area-chart {
  height: 200px;
}
```

To complete it—the most important part for this card—create the function calls in the JavaScript:

```
$('#daily-usage .area-chart').highcharts({
    title: {
        text: '',
    },
    tooltip: {
        pointFormat: '{series.name}:
<b>{point.percentage:.1f}%</b>'
    },
    plotOptions: {
        pie: {
            dataLabels: {
                enabled: true,
                style: {
                    fontWeight: '300'
                }
            }
        }
    },
    series: [{
        type: 'pie',
        name: 'Time share',
        data: [
            ['Front yard', 10.38],
            ['Closet', 26.33],
            ['Swim pool', 51.03],
            ['Like a boss', 4.77],
            ['Barking', 3.93]
        ]
    }]
});
```

As you can see in the preceding code, we set the graph to be of the pie type and create the share for each segment in the data array.

The following screenshot shows how the last card must be displayed on the web browser:

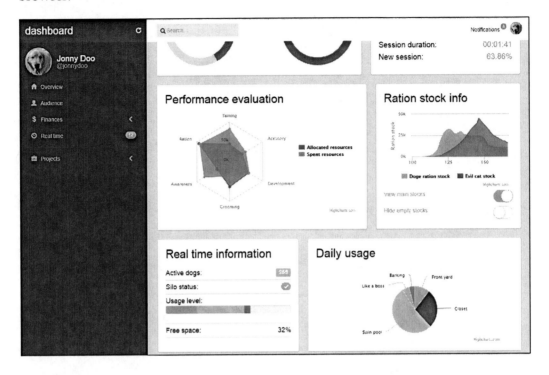

And we are done! The main page of the dashboard is complete. Now let's proceed to the next pages in this component.

Fixing the mobile viewport

If you resize the dashboard to a mobile visualization (treated as an extra-small viewport in Bootstrap,) you should see some problems with the elements that are not appearing correctly. As shown in the next screenshot, note that the search appears and the card with the round chart is completely unaligned.

In this visualization mode, we are using the viewport of iPhone 6 in portrait orientation in the Chrome developer inspector:

Regarding the search bar, it will be better if this bar appears just when required, for example, when clicking on a button. So, next to the refresh button, let's create another icon to toggle the search bar.

The HTML for this section must be like the following code:

```html
<div class="col-sm-3 top-left-menu">
  <div class="navbar-header">
    <a class="navbar-brand" href="dashboard.html">
      <h1>dashboard</h1>
    </a>

    <button type="button" class="navbar-toggle collapsed" data-
toggle="collapse" data-target="#nav-menu" aria-expanded="false">
      <span class="sr-only">Toggle navigation</span>
      <span class="icon-bar"></span>
      <span class="icon-bar"></span>
      <span class="icon-bar"></span>
    </button>
  </div>
  <a href="#" id="search-icon" data-toggle="tooltip" data-
placement="bottom" data-delay="500" title="Display search bar"
class="header-buttons pull-right visible-xs">
    <span class="glyphicon glyphicon-search" aria-hidden="true"></
span>
  </a>
  <a href="#" data-toggle="tooltip" data-placement="bottom" data-
delay="500" title="Refresh data" class="header-buttons pull-right">
    <span class="glyphicon glyphicon-repeat" aria-hidden="true"></
span>
  </a>
</div>
```

Let's discuss this code. First, we made a change in the class name. The link in the refresh icon was a `.header-refresh`. Now, since we have multiple header buttons, we changed it to a `.header-button` class for generalization.

We also added the Bootstrap tooltip for this button, just as we did for the refresh icon, displaying the message: `"Display search bar"`.

To complete the changes, replace the class names in the CSS as well:

```css
nav .header-buttons {
  margin-left: auto;
  color: #FFF;
}
```

Then the header should look like this:

Now we have to fix the search bar. Let's change the classes on the `form#search`.
Replace the classes from `.hidden-sm.col-md-3` to just `.col-sm-3` for better
visualization.

 Remember the gridding foundations? By setting the `form` for this class, it
will fill 3 out of 12 columns in the template until the small viewports and
appear as a line block for extra small viewports.

Now, let's hide the form using a media query in CSS for extra small viewports:

```
@media (max-width:48em) {
  form#search {
    display: none;
  }
}
```

To toggle the visualization of the search input, let's add some JavaScript events. The
first one is for opening the search when we click on the magnifier icon at the header,
identified by `#search-icon`. So in our `main.js` file, we add the following function:

```
$('#search-icon').on('click', function(e) {
    e.preventDefault();
    $('form#search').slideDown('fast');
    $('form#search input:first').focus();
});
```

What this will do first is prevent the default click action with the
`e.preventDefault()` caller. Then, we use the `.slideDown` function from jQuery,
which slides down an element. In this case, it will toggle `form#search`.

After toggling the form, we add focus to the input, which will open the keyboard if
we are accessing the page from a mobile phone.

To increment that, it would be nice if the search bar can hide when the user blurs the focus on the search input. To do this, add the following event handler to the JavaScript:

```
$('form#search input').on('blur', function(e) {
    if($('#search-icon').is(':visible')) {
        $('form#search').slideUp('fast');
    }
});
```

What we are doing here is using the `blur` event, which is triggered whenever the element loses the focus. The trigger performs a check to find out whether the `#search-icon` is visible, meaning that we are in the extra small viewport, and then hides the search bar using the `slideUp` function, doing the opposite of what the `slideDown` function does.

Fixing the navigation menu

Click on the collapse toggle navigation (the hamburger button) and you will see how the `#nav-menu` looks so messy, as shown in the next screenshot. We must fix it just like the way we did in the last web application example:

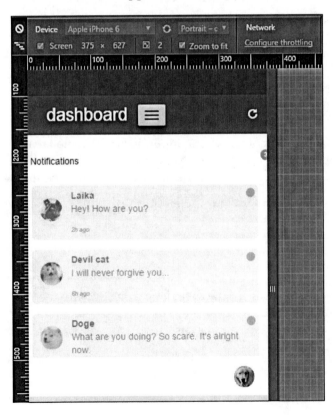

To do this, we will first need to remove the `.pull-right` class from `#nav-menu`. The `.pull-*` classes add a float to the element by applying the `!important` flag, which cannot be overridden. In this case, we must override this style rule to remove the `.pull-right` class and add the float to the current element style rule:

```
#nav-menu {
    float: right;
}
```

Create a media query for extra small devices for `#nav-menu` and remove the `float: right`:

```
@media (max-width:48em) {
    #nav-menu {
        float: none;
    }
}
```

After that, we must hide `#nav-profile` and move its button to the `#nav-menu` list. First, add the `.hidden-xs` class to the profile element:

```
<div id="nav-profile" class="btn-group pull-right hidden-xs">
    ...
</div>
```

This will prevent the element from appearing for extra small devices using the Bootstrap viewport helper class. Then, in `#nav-menu > ul`, append the options that were in the `#nav-profile` drop-down button:

```
<div id="nav-menu" class="collapse navbar-collapse">
  <ul class="nav navbar-nav">
    <li>...</li>
    <li class="visible-xs">
      <a href="#">Profile</a>
    </li>
    <li class="visible-xs">
      <a href="settings.html">Setting</a>
    </li>
    <li class="visible-xs">
      <a href="#">Logout</a>
    </li>
  </ul>
</div>
```

Note that we make this new item list visible only for extra small viewports with the `.visible-xs` class.

These new item lists must now look just like the notification one, already present in this list. So, append the selector of the new item list to the current CSS style of `#btn-notification`:

```
#btn-notifications .btn-link,
#nav-menu li a {
  padding-top: 1.5rem;
  color: #252830;
  font-weight: 500;
}
```

The opened list should look like this:

Now, try to change the viewport and see how the elements on the header correctly change its visualization. The `#nav-profile` will appear only for small-to-large viewports and will shrink into `#nav-menu ul` in a small visualization for extra small viewports.

The notification list needs some style

If you click on the notification list to open it, you will see three problems: firstly, the badge holding the number of new notifications jumps to the right portion; then the notification button is not filling the entire width; and finally, the notification list can appear a little nicer when opened.

To fix the jumping badge on the notification button, just add the following CSS:

```
@media (max-width:48em) {
  #nav-menu #btn-notifications > .badge {
    right: inherit;
    left: 10rem;
  }
}
```

Note that we use a media query to change the position of the badge for extra small viewports only.

To modify the notification button's width, we have to create a media query as well. So, add this CSS style to it:

```
@media (max-width:48em) {
  #btn-notifications,
  #btn-notifications > button {
    width: 100%;
    text-align: left;
  }
}
```

This style will change the width for both the notification button dropdown and the button itself.

Finally, the style for the notification list must be changed. We create the next CSS rule in our `main.css` file, and it should instantly look good:

```
@media (max-width:48em) {
  #notification-list {
    margin: 1.25rem;
    margin-left: 2rem;
    background-color: #e5e9ec;
  }

  #notification-list a {
    background-color: #FFF;
    opacity: 1;
  }
}
```

Awesome! Update your web browser and `#notification-list` should look like what is shown in this screenshot:

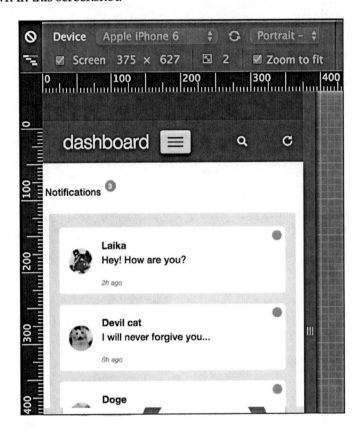

Adding the missing left menu

Where are the items of the left menu? If you check out the HTML of `#side-menu`, you will see that we have added the `.hidden-xs` class to it. So, we must move the navigation options to another place in this extra small viewport.

Let's add the links to `#nav-menu` `ul` just as we did for `#nav-profile`:

```html
<div id="nav-menu" class="collapse navbar-collapse">
  <ul class="nav navbar-nav">
    <li>...</li>
    <li class="visible-xs">
      <a href="#">Audience</a>
    </li>
    <li class="visible-xs">
      <a href="#">Finances</a>
    </li>
    <li class="visible-xs">
      <a href="#">Realtime</a>
    </li>
    <li class="visible-xs">
      <a href="#">Projects</a>
    </li>

    <li role="separator" class="divider visible-xs"></li>
    ...
  </ul>
</div>
```

Modify the maximum height of `#nav-menu` when collapse is toggled with the style:

```css
#nav-menu.navbar-collapse {
  max-height: 39rem;
}
```

For the `.divider` element in the list, create the following CSS:

```css
#nav-menu .divider {
  height: 0.1rem;
  margin: 0.9rem 0;
  overflow: hidden;
  background-color: #e5e5e5;
}
```

Notice that in #nav-menu ul, the notification button will appear above the new elements added and the options from #nav-profile will appear below. The next screenshot represents the visualization of the final arrangement of the #nav-menu toggle:

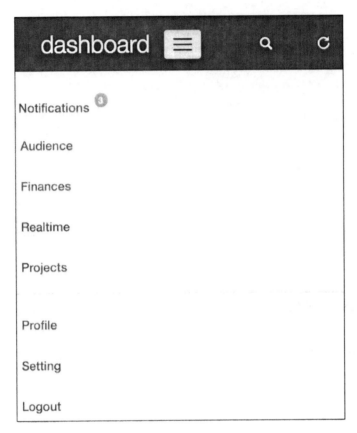

Aligning the round charts

The .round-charts inside the #pie-charts element does not appear correctly aligned. However, we can quickly fix this with two CSS rules using media queries. So, create the following style:

```
@media(max-width:48em){
  .round-chart,
  .round-chart canvas {
    display: block;
    margin: auto;
  }
}
```

```
.round-chart + .round-chart {
  margin-top: 2rem;
  float: none;
  }
}
```

Refresh the web page and see the result, like the following screenshot:

Great! Now we have our dashboard nailed for every viewport and device! That was a thorough task, but with a great payoff, because we have now created a complete dashboard. Let's move forward to some other pages in our example.

Learning more advanced plugins

Now that we have created the main page of the dashboard example and nailed almost every element, plugin, and component in Bootstrap, let's use some other advanced JavaScript plugins to complete our journey.

For this part, let's create another file named `audience.html` in the same folder of `dashboard.html`. In this file, copy the exact same code of `dashboard.html`, except the HTML inside the `div#main` element, because that is where we will make some new changes.

Using the Bootstrap carousel

Bootstrap provides us with a nice plugin to slideshow components through cycling elements, although it's pretty verbose and a little complicated to understand at first sight.

First of all, we need to create an element inside our `div#main`:

```
<div id="main" class="col-sm-offset-3 col-sm-9">
  <div id="carousel-notification" class="carousel" data-
ride="carousel">
      ...
  </div>
</div>
```

We must identify this element for the Bootstrap Carousel plugin, so we have called it `#carousel-notification` at our outmost `div` of the plugin.

Bootstrap will start a carousel via the data attributes for elements marked with `data-ride="carousel"`, just like our element. In addition, this element must have the `.carousel` class for the CSS style.

We must create the elements inside the slides for the carousel, so we use the following markup to create the notification slides:

```
<div id="main" class="col-sm-offset-3 col-sm-9">
  <div id="carousel-notification" class="carousel" data-
ride="carousel">
    <div class="carousel-inner" role="listbox">
      <div class="item active">
        <img src="imgs/doge.jpg" width="512">
        <div class="carousel-caption">
          <p>What are you doing? So scare. It's alright now.</p>
        </div>
      </div>
      <div class="item">
```

```
      <img src="imgs/cat.jpg" width="512">
      <div class="carousel-caption">
        <p>I will never forgive you...</p>
      </div>
    </div>
    <div class="item">
      <img src="imgs/laika.jpg" width="512">
      <div class="carousel-caption">
        <p>Hey! How are you?</p>
      </div>
    </div>
  </div>
 </div>
</div>
```

Note that we have created three items. Each item has been created inside the .carousel-inner element. Inside this element, the items have been created with the .item class.

Inside each .item, there is an image followed by another element with the .carousel-caption class, which contains text to be displayed as captions for each slide. Note that the first slide also contains the .active class, which must necessarily be added to one (and only one) of the slides.

At this point, refresh Bootstrap carousel your browser and you should see the page like what is shown in this screenshot:

If you wait 5 seconds, you will see the image and caption change. You can set this interval value by the `data-interval` data attribute or through JavaScript, as an initializer parameter, as shown in this example:

```
$('.carousel').carousel({
  interval: 1000 // value in milliseconds
})
```

Also observe that there is no animation between the changes of the slides. To add it, put the `.slide` class into the `.carousel` element and you will see a left slide of the images.

Remember that versions 8 and 9 of Internet Explorer do not support CSS animations. Therefore, the Bootstrap carousel plugin will work unless you add transition fallbacks on your own, such as jQuery animations.

Customizing carousel items

For each item in the carousel, we just created a simple `<p>` element inside it. However, you can add other elements, as in the following example, where we are adding a heading 3:

```
<div class="item">
  <img src="imgs/laika.jpg" width="512">
  <div class="carousel-caption">
    <h3>Laika said:</h3>
    <p>Hey! How are you?</p>
  </div>
</div>
```

Creating slide indicators

The Bootstrap carousel also offers the ability to create bullet slide indicators. To do this, add the following code after the `.carousel-inner` element:

```
<div id="carousel-notification" class="carousel slide" data-
ride="carousel">
  <div class="carousel-inner" role="listbox">
    ...
  </div>
```

```
<!-- Indicators -->
<ol class="carousel-indicators">
  <li data-target="#carousel-notification" data-slide-to="0"
class="active"></li>
  <li data-target="#carousel-notification" data-slide-to="1"></li>
  <li data-target="#carousel-notification" data-slide-to="2"></li>
</ol>
</div>
```

We just created an ordered list, `<ol>`. On each item, we have to say which is the carousel element identifier through `data-target` (in this case, it is `#carousel-notification`) and which slide each bullet will correspond to through `data-slide-to`. To do this, we just create the number of list items from the same size of the image items and enumerate them.

Refresh the browser, and now you should see the carousel with the bullets and all the modifications (the slide transition, the heading on the image item, and the bullet identifier), like this:

Adding navigation controls

Another cool option in the Bootstrap carousel is creating side navigation controls to change slides from left to right.

We add the markup for this after the indicator's one, as shown in the following HTML code:

```html
<div id="carousel-notification" class="carousel slide" data-ride="carousel">
  <div class="carousel-inner" role="listbox">
    ...
  </div>

  <!-- Indicators -->
  <ol class="carousel-indicators">
  </ol>

  <!-- Controls -->
  <a class="left carousel-control" href="#carousel-notification" role="button" data-slide="prev">
    <span class="glyphicon glyphicon-chevron-left" aria-hidden="true"></span>
    <span class="sr-only">Previous</span>
  </a>
  <a class="right carousel-control" href="#carousel-notification" role="button" data-slide="next">
    <span class="glyphicon glyphicon-chevron-right" aria-hidden="true"></span>
    <span class="sr-only">Next</span>
  </a>
</div>
```

As you can see, we created two carousel controls, one to the right and one to the left. Each of them must be inside an `<a>` tag identified by the `.carousel-control` class and the class for the action, which is `.right` or `.left`.

The `href` of the element represents the identifier of the carousel, just as `data-target` in the bullet indicators. The `data-slide` indicates the action that should be performed by the control, which can be `next` to move to the next slide or `prev` to move to the previous slide.

The next screenshot presents the final expected result of the carousel:

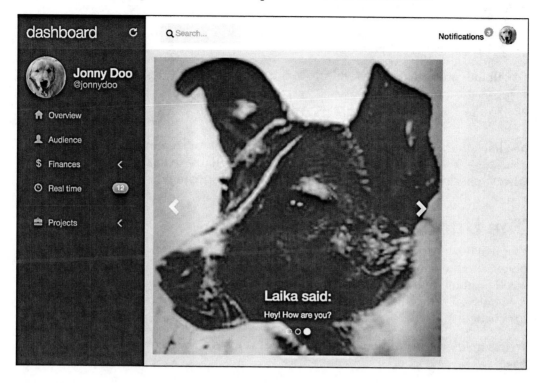

> **Using multiple Bootstrap carousels on the same page**
>
>
> If you plan to use multiple Bootstrap carousels on the same page, remember to correctly apply a unique id to the parent element (the one with the `.carousel` class). Also remember to update the target for the bullet indicator and slide controls.

Other methods and options for the carousel

Just like every Bootstrap plugin, the carousel offers a set of parameters and methods that can be used. Check out the official documentation for detailed info (`http://getbootstrap.com/javascript/#carousel-options`).

There are some options that we should be talking about, such as `wrap`, which defines whether the carousel should be cyclic or not. By default, this option has the value `true`.

You can also call via JavaScript to the carousel go to a certain slide or just force a slide switch. To go to a certain slide, use this function:

```
$('.carousel').carousel(2); // which 2 is the slide enumerated as
2 in the data-slide-to
```

To call the carousel to switch slides, use the same function but pass the prev or next string as the argument:

```
$('.carousel').carousel('next') // or 'prev'
```

Just like other Bootstrap plugins, the carousel is great for creating slide images on your page. There are a plenty of customizations available to fit the required styles. Always check out the documentation for further information.

The Bootstrap spy

You will now learn another Bootstrap plugin—Bootstrap Scrollspy. Scrollspy is a plugin used to automatically update any kind of Bootstrap navigation based on the scroll position. Many sites use it, including the Bootstrap documentation, in the side navigation. There, when you scroll the page, the active elements in the navigation bar change.

To exemplify the utilization of the plugin, let's create a .card on our audience.html page:

```
<div class="card">
  <div class="card-block">

  </div>
</div>
```

Inside .card-block, we will create two columns, the left one for the spy navigation and one to the right for the content itself. Remember to always place your .col-*-* inside a .row element:

```
<div class="card">
  <div class="card-block">
    <div class="row">
      <div class="col-sm-3" id="content-spy"></div>
      <div id="content" class="col-sm-9"></div>
    </div>
  </div>
</div>
```

We are identifying the navigation column as #content-spy and the content column as just #content.

First, let's create the left navigation using the .nav-pills.nav-stacked Bootstrap component. Do you remember it? Let's refresh your memory by using it again, as follows:

```
<div class="card">
  <div class="card-block">
    <div class="row">
      <div class="col-sm-3" id="content-spy">
        <ul class="nav nav-pills nav-stacked">
          <li role="presentation" class="active">
            <a href="#lorem">The Lorem</a>
          </li>
          <li role="presentation">
            <a href="#eros">The Eros</a>
          </li>
          <li role="presentation">
            <a href="#vestibulum">The Vestibulum</a>
          </li>
        </ul>
      </div>
      <div id="content" class="col-sm-9"></div>
    </div>
  </div>
</div>
```

All we need to do is create a <ul> with the .nav, .nav-pills, and .nav-stacked classes. Then we create three item lists, each one with a link inside, referencing an ID in the HTML (#lorem, #eros, and #vestibulum). We will use these IDs later to refer to the Scrollspy.

Now create the content. It must be in the #content three <div>, each one with the ID corresponding to the references in the href of the link in the item list, as shown in this code:

```
<div class="card">
  <div class="card-block">
    <div class="row">
      <div class="col-sm-3" id="content-spy">
        <ul class="nav nav-pills nav-stacked">
          <li role="presentation" class="active">
            <a href="#lorem">The Lorem</a>
          </li>
```

```
        <li role="presentation">
          <a href="#eros">The Eros</a>
        </li>
        <li role="presentation">
          <a href="#vestibulum">The Vestibulum</a>
        </li>
      </ul>
    </div>
    <div id="content" class="col-sm-9">
      <div id="lorem">
        <h2>The Lorem</h2>
        <p>
          Lorem ipsum dolor sit amet… <!-- Rest of the text -->
        </p>
      </div>
      <div id="eros">
        <h2>The Eros</h2>
        <p>
          Curabitur eget pharetra risus… <!-- Rest of the text -->
        </p>
      </div>
      <div id="vestibulum">
        <h2>The Vestibulum</h2>
        <p>
          Integer eleifend consectetur… <!-- Rest of the text -->
          <img src="imgs/jon.png" class="img-responsive">
        </p>
      </div>
    </div>
   </div>
  </div>
 </div>
```

Note the identifiers on each <div> corresponding to the href in the link of the item list. This is used to correlate the scroll with the active item in the nav element.

 Do not forget to add the .img-responsive class to the image at the end of the third content item.

To activate the plugin, we have two options. Activate it by data attributes or by JavaScript. If you choose JavaScript, place the call function in main.js:

```
$('#content').scrollspy({
  target: '#content-spy'
})
```

Refresh the page and see it working. If you want to use data attributes, place a data-spy and a data-target in the #content element:

```
<div class="card">
  <div class="card-block">
    <div class="row">
      <div class="col-sm-3" id="content-spy">
        <ul class="nav nav-pills nav-stacked">
          <li role="presentation" class="active">
          <a href="#lorem">The Lorem</a>
          </li>
          <li role="presentation">
            <a href="#eros">The Eros</a>
          </li>
          <li role="presentation">
            <a href="#vestibulum">The Vestibulum</a>
          </li>
        </ul>
      </div>
      <div id="content" class="col-sm-9" data-spy="scroll" data-target="#content-spy">
        <div id="lorem">
          <h2>The Lorem</h2>
          <p>
            Lorem ipsum dolor sit amet… <!-- Rest of the text -->
          </p>
        </div>
        <div id="eros">
          <h2>The Eros</h2>
          <p>
            Curabitur eget pharetra risus… <!-- Rest of the text -->
          </p>
        </div>
        <div id="vestibulum">
          <h2>The Vestibulum</h2>
          <p>
```

```
            Integer eleifend consectetur… <!-- Rest of the text -->
            <img src="imgs/jon.png" class="img-responsive">
          </p>
        </div>
      </div>
    </div>
  </div>
</div>
```

The data-spy must have the scroll value in order to identify that the spy must be active for the scrolling action. The data-target works just like the parameter target passed in the activation by JavaScript. It should represent the element that will spy on the element, #content-spy in this case.

To make a final effect for the scrolling, create the following CSS to limit the height and adjust the scroll of the content:

```
#content {
  height: 30em;
  overflow: auto;
}
```

Refresh your web browser and the card should appear like what is shown in the next screenshot. Note that here we have scrolled the content to the second item.

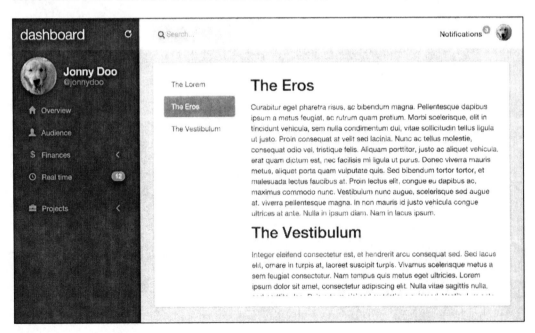

Great! Now you have learned another Bootstrap plugin! The Scrollspy plugin is very useful, especially on pages with extensive content, subdivided into sections. Make great use of it.

Summary

In this chapter, we greatly finished our dashboard example. We had to create some cards from the last chapter and adjust the visualization for any viewport. The result is a great dashboard that can be used in multiple contexts and web applications.

The user experience and the visuals of the dashboard were impressive in the end, creating a desirable page for this kind of application that works on any device.

Then we moved forward to explain some more Bootstrap plugins. We analyzed Bootstrap Scrollspy, which is a great plugin for you when you are creating pages with large content and need to summarize the sections while the user is scrolling. We used this plugin just with sample content, but remember to use it whenever needed.

We analyzed the Bootstrap carousel as well. The carousel is a great plugin for making slides of images with caption text. In my opinion, the only downside to this plugin is that it is too much typed. Imagine if we could create the same carousel using lines of code. I think we can fix that in the last chapter!

In the next chapter, we will start a plugin customization and use the carousel as an example. We can create a kind of wrapper to reduce typing of the carousel and automate plugin creation. Also, we will go deep into some Bootstrap plugin customizations.

For sure, it will be another challenge to create a plugin for Bootstrap, but I am confident that we can nail that as well.

11
Making It Your Taste

At this point, you can be called a Bootstrap master around the world! You nailed the framework as few people do these days—you should be proud of that!

Now, you are about to face a challenge to overpass the boundaries of learning. In this chapter, we will see how to create and customize your own Bootstrap plugin. This could be tough, but if you reached this point you can go a step further to become a true Bootstrap master.

The topics covered are as follows:

- Customizing Bootstrap components
- Customizing Bootstrap plugins
- Creating a Bootstrap plugin

When we finish this chapter, we will also reach the end of the book. I hope this last chapter will help you empower yourself with all the Bootstrap framework skills.

To follow this chapter, create a `sandbox.html` file and just place the default template that we are using all over the book. We will place all the code snippets of this chapter in this file.

Customizing a Bootstrap component

In my years of experience of using Bootstrap, one of the major issues that I received is how can I change a Bootstrap component to appear like I need?

Most of the time, the answer is to take a look at the CSS and see how you can override the style. However, this orientation can be obscure sometimes and the developer will be unable to find a solution.

In this section, we will customize some Bootstrap components. We did some of that in previous chapters, but now we will go a step further into this subject. Let's start customizing a single button.

The taste of your button

We must start with a button, because of two factors. First, it is a quite simple component and second we have to customize a button very often.

Let's assume we have a simple button placed in a page that already has the Bootstrap fully loaded. We will call it as the sandbox page. The HTML for it should be like this:

```
<button type="button" class="btn btn-primary" aria-pressed="false"
autocomplete="off">
   This is a simple button
</button>
```

As we saw so many times, this button is a simple one with the `.btn` and `.btn-default` classes that will make the button blue, as shown in the next screenshot:

If you want a different color for the button, you can use one of the others contextual classes provided by Bootstrap (`.btn-success`, `.btn-info`, `.btn-warning`, `.btn-danger`, and so on) by using them together with the base class `.btn` class.

If you want to define a new color, the suggestion is to create a new class and define the necessary pseudo-class. Let's assume we want a purple button defined by a class `.btn-purple`. Define a CSS for it:

```
.btn-purple {
    color: #fff;
    background-color: #803BDB;
    border-color: #822FBA;
}
```

This is the base CSS. Now we must define all the pseudo-classes for the button:

```css
.btn-purple:hover,
.btn-purple:focus,
.btn-purple:active,
.btn-purple.active {
    color: #ffffff;
    background-color: #6B39AD;
    border-color: #822FBA;
}
```

Now, for every interaction with the button (such as hovering over it), the button will have a background color a little darker. Not all same pseudo-classes can have the same style; you can customize it as per your choice.

The next screenshot represents our new button. What we did was replace the `.btn-default` for the class `.btn-purple`. The one on the left is `.btn-purple` and the one on the right is `.btn-purple:hover`:

Using button toggle

Bootstrap has a nice feature for button toggle. It is native from the framework and can be used in different ways. We will take a look at the single toggle button. For that, create a normal button in the sandbox page:

```html
<button type="button" class="btn btn-primary" autocomplete="off">
  Single toggle
</button>
```

To make this button turn into a single toggle, we have to add the data attribute `data-toggle="button"` and the attribute `aria-pressed="true"`. This will turn the button into a toggle button. Now when you click on the button, Bootstrap will add a class `.active` to it, making it appear pressed. The code is as follows:

```html
<button type="button" class="btn btn-default" data-toggle="button"
aria-pressed="false" autocomplete="off">
  Single toggle
</button>
```

The checkbox toggle buttons

The toggle buttons can turn into buttons checkbox or buttons radio. At first, we need to remember the concept of button group. So let's create a simple `.btn-group` in the HTML:

```
<div class="btn-group">
  <button class="btn btn-default">
    Laika
  </button>
  <button class="btn btn-default">
    Jonny
  </button>
  <button class="btn btn-default">
    Doge
  </button>
</div>
```

The concept of using button groups is to create a `div` with the class `.btn-group` and insert a bunch of `button` elements inside it. However, we want a bunch of checkboxes, so let's substitute the `button` element for a `label` and `input` elements with type `checkbox`:

```
<div class="btn-group">
  <label class="btn btn-default">
    <input type="checkbox" autocomplete="off"> Laika
  </label>
  <label class="btn btn-default">
    <input type="checkbox" autocomplete="off"> Jonny
  </label>
  <label class="btn btn-default">
    <input type="checkbox" autocomplete="off"> Doge
  </label>
</div>
```

Refresh the page and you will see that the button list now has a checkbox input on each label, as shown in the following screenshot:

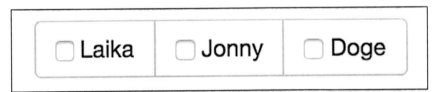

To change it to toggle and hide the checkboxes, we just need to simple add the data attribute `data-toggle="buttons"`.

There is an option to preselect a checkbox, just need to add the `.active` class to the label and add the attribute `checked="checked"` to the input:

```
<div class="btn-group" data-toggle="buttons">
  <label class="btn btn-default">
    <input type="checkbox" autocomplete="off"> Laika
  </label>
  <label class="btn btn-default active">
    <input type="checkbox" autocomplete="off" checked="checked">
Jonny
  </label>
  <label class="btn btn-default">
    <input type="checkbox" autocomplete="off"> Doge
  </label>
</div>
```

The next image shows the final output of the checkbox with the second checkbox selected on the page reload:

The button as a radio button

The other option for the toggle button is to become a radio button. The procedure is very similar to the checkbox. We just need to change the input from `type="checkbox"` to `type="radio"`:

```
<div class="btn-group" data-toggle="buttons">
  <label class="btn btn-default">
    <input type="radio" autocomplete="off"> Laika
  </label>
  <label class="btn btn-default active">
    <input type="radio" autocomplete="off" checked="checked"> Jonny
  </label>
  <label class="btn btn-default">
    <input type="radio" autocomplete="off"> Doge
  </label>
</div>
```

This will create a `.btn-group` formed by radio button, been just one selected at once.

Doing the JavaScript customization

Buttons can be customized using JavaScript as well. For instance, any toggle button can be toggled by calling:

```
$('button selector').button('toggle')
```

This will toggle the state of the button from active to not active.

Before Version 3.3.6, it was possible to change the text of a button via JavaScript by calling the button passing a string. First, you should define a state text. For instance, let's define a button with the attribute `data-statesample-text="What a sample"`:

```
<button type="button" class="btn btn-primary" autocomplete="off"
data-statesample-text="What a sample">
  Single toggle
</button>
```

Using JavaScript, you can change the text with the value or the data text by calling:

```
$('button').button('statesample');
```

Reset the text to original with the following function:

```
$('button').button('reset');
```

However, this feature is deprecated after Version 3.3.6 and will be removed in Version 4 of Bootstrap.

Working with plugin customization

Just like the customization for components, it is also possible to customize the behavior of the Bootstrap plugins.

To illustrate that, let's consider the Bootstrap Modal. This plugin is one of the most used among the others. The Modal is able to create a separated flow in your web page without changing the context.

Let's create an input and a button and make the button open the modal when clicked. What we are expecting here is when the user inputs the GitHub username at the input, we will get the info in the GitHub open API and show some basic info at the Modal. For this, create the following code in the sandbox page:

```
<!-- Button trigger modal -->
<input id="github-username" type="text" class="form-control"
placeholder="Type your github username here">
<button type="button" class="btn btn-success btn-lg btn-block"
data-toggle="modal" data-target="#githubModal">
  Launch demo modal
</button>

<!-- Modal -->
<div class="modal fade" id="githubModal" tabindex="-1"
role="dialog">
  <div class="modal-dialog" role="document">
    <div class="modal-content">
      <div class="modal-header">
        <button type="button" class="close" data-dismiss="modal"
aria-label="Close"><span aria-hidden="true">&times;</span></button>
        <h4 class="modal-title"></h4>
      </div>
      <div class="modal-body">
      </div>
      <div class="modal-footer">
        <button type="button" class="btn btn-default" data-
dismiss="modal">Close</button>
        <button type="button" class="btn btn-success">Save
changes</button>
      </div>
    </div>
  </div>
</div>
```

Refresh the web page and you will see the input followed by a button. When you click on it, the Modal will show. The Modal is completely empty; to interact with that, we will play with some JavaScript.

In the code, let's use the Bootstrap event `show.bs.modal`, which will be triggered whenever a Modal is shown (like we discussed previously):

```
$('#githubModal).on('show.bs.modal', function (e) {
    var $element = $(this),
        url = 'https://api.github.com/users/{username}';
});
```

Inside the function, we defined two variables. The `$element` corresponds to the triggered element, in this case it is the modal `#githubModal`. The `url` is the endpoint for the GitHub API. We will replace the `{username}` parameter on the string based on the text passed at the input by doing that:

```
$('#githubModal).on('show.bs.modal', function (e) {
    var $element = $(this),
        url = 'https://api.github.com/users/{username}';

    url = url.replace(/{username}/, $('#github-username').val());
});
```

Then, we must make a request to the API to retrieve the user info. To do so, we must make a GET request to the API, which will return us a JSON.

To make it clear, JSON is an open standard format to transmit data as a set of key-values. It is widely used to transfer data from web services and APIs, such as GitHub.

Moving on, to make the request to the server, we use the function `$.get` from jQuery. Pass a URL and a callback function with the JSON `data` object returned from the server:

```
$('#githubModal').on('show.bs.modal', function (e) {
    var $element = $(this),
        url = 'https://api.github.com/users/{username}';

    $.get(url, function(data) {
        console.log(data);
    });
});
```

If everything is working so far, refresh your web browser, type your username on the input, and click on the button. After the modal opens, check your console terminal and you must see the data from the request, as shown in the following screenshot:

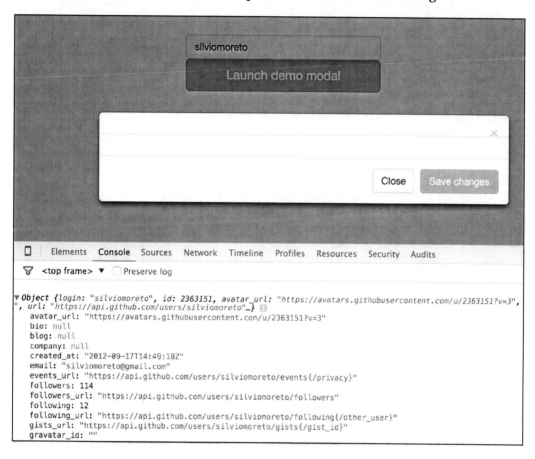

Now, it would be good if we parse the data and displayed some information on the modal. For that, let's use the same principle for replace the url variable. Along with the variables, let's add other ones related to the template.

We want to create a template with two columns, the left one the user avatar image from the object and some basic info on the right. So, add the highlighted lines in your JavaScript:

```
$('#githubModal').on('show.bs.modal', function (e) {
    var $element = $(this),
        url = 'https://api.github.com/users/{username}',
        title = 'Hi, my name is {name}',
        content = '' +
            '<div class="row">' +
                '<img src="{img}" class="col-sm-3">' +
                '<p class="col-sm-9" id="bio">{bio}</p>' +
            '</div>',

        bio = '' +
            'At moment I have {publicRepo} public repos ' +
            'and {followers} followers.\n' +
            'I joined Github on {dateJoin}';

    $.get(url, function(data) {
        console.log(data);
    });
});
```

Here, we created three template variables that we will replace with the data from the get request. Inside the get function, let's replace the variables and create our final template.

The principle is the same as what we applied to the url, just replace the key, which is surrounded by curly brackets, with the value on data:

```
$('#githubModal').on('show.bs.modal', function (e) {
    var $element = $(this),
        url = 'https://api.github.com/users/{username}',
        title = 'Hi, my name is {name}',
        content = '' +
            '<div class="row">' +
                '<img src="{img}" class="col-sm-3">' +
                '<p class="col-sm-9" id="bio">{bio}</p>' +
            '</div>',
```

```
        bio = '' +
            'At moment I have {publicRepo} public repos ' +
            'and {followers} followers.\n' +
            'I joined Github on {dateJoin}';

    url = url.replace(/{username}/, $('#github-username').val());

    $.get(url, function(data) {
        title = title.replace(/{name}/, data.name);

        bio = bio.replace(/{publicRepo}/, data.public_repos)
                .replace(/{followers}/, data.followers)
                .replace(/{dateJoin}/, data.created_at.split('T')
    [0]);

        content = content.replace(/{img}/, data.avatar_url)
                        .replace(/{bio}/, bio);

        $element.find('.modal-title').text(title);
        $element.find('.modal-body').html(content);
    });
});
```

After all the replacements, we set the parsed template variables to the modal. We query the title to find the `.modal-title` and insert the text inside, while we insert the HTML for `.modal-body`.

The difference here is that we can pass an HTML or a simple text to jQuery. Take care when you pass an HTML to ensure that your HTML is not degenerated. That might cause issues for your client. So, pay attention when you want to set just a text, like for `.modal-title`, or a valid `html`, like for `.modal-body`.

On the browser, type your GitHub username on the input, press the button, and you should see a nice modal, such as the one in the next screenshot:

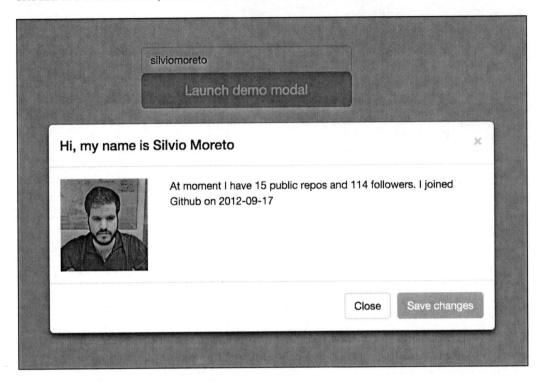

So, we saw how to interact more with the Bootstrap plugins while customizing it for our own tasty.

Remember that the Bootstrap events exist for every Bootstrap plugin. They are friendly and can be very handy while interacting with the plugins, like in this case, to execute some action when the Modal shows.

The additional Bootstrap plugins

Bootstrap has plugins for almost anything. However, there are some missing components and plugins that would be nice to have in our web pages, for example, a data picker, or a color picker, or a select component. Bootstrap does not incorporate these plugins into the framework because they are not that generic for any application, so you should add it if you need.

Knowing that, the Bootstrap developers provide a list of additional Bootstrap resources that can be found at `http://expo.getbootstrap.com/resources/`.

Creating our Bootstrap plugin

In the previous chapter, we discussed the Carousel Bootstrap plugin. Do you remember the HTML markup to use the plugin? It is a big markup as you can see from the following code:

```html
<div id="carousel-notification" class="carousel slide" data-ride="carousel">

  <!-- Wrapper for slides -->
  <div class="carousel-inner" role="listbox">
    <div class="item active">
      <img src="imgs/doge.jpg" width="512">
      <div class="carousel-caption">
        <h3>Doge said:</h3>
        <p>What are you doing? So scare. It's alright now.</p>
      </div>
    </div>
    <div class="item">
      <img src="imgs/cat.jpg" width="512">
      <div class="carousel-caption">
        <h3>Crazy cat said:</h3>
        <p>I will never forgive you...</p>
      </div>
    </div>
    <div class="item">
      <img src="imgs/laika.jpg" width="512">
      <div class="carousel-caption">
        <h3>Laika said:</h3>
        <p>Hey! How are you?</p>
      </div>
    </div>
  </div>

  <!-- Indicators -->
  <ol class="carousel-indicators">
    <li data-target="#carousel-notification" data-slide-to="0" class="active"></li>
    <li data-target="#carousel-notification" data-slide-to="1"></li>
    <li data-target="#carousel-notification" data-slide-to="2"></li>
  </ol>
```

```
    <!-- Controls -->
    <a class="left carousel-control" href="#carousel-notification"
role="button" data-slide="prev">
        <span class="glyphicon glyphicon-chevron-left" aria-
hidden="true"></span>
        <span class="sr-only">Previous</span>
    </a>
    <a class="right carousel-control" href="#carousel-notification"
role="button" data-slide="next">
        <span class="glyphicon glyphicon-chevron-right" aria-
hidden="true"></span>
        <span class="sr-only">Next</span>
    </a>
</div>
```

There is a reason why the plugin has all these lines of code. With all of that, you are able to customize the plugin for your own use. However, it would be nice if we had a simple carousel with fewer lines of code. Can we do that?

The template that we are trying to create for new plugin will have only the HTML that will reflect the same action as the preceding code:

```
<div id="carousel-notification" class="bootstrap-carousel">
  <img src="imgs/doge.jpg" data-title="doge" data-content="Hey
there!">
  <img src="imgs/laika.jpg" data-title="laika" data-content="Hey
...!">
  <img src="imgs/cat.jpg" data-title="cat">
</div>
```

In the plugin, we will have only one `div` wrapping up everything. Inside that, we will have a sequence of `img` elements, each one containing the image source, the title via `data-title`, and the slide content via `data-content`.

Building a plugin from scratch is quite difficult, but we will be able to learn the concepts behind Bootstrap and master it when we finish the plugin.

Creating the plugin scaffold

First of all, let's define the directories and files that we are using. For the HTML, we will start a new one that will have the same base template that was used in all the other examples.

Inside the `imgs` directory, we will keep the pet images that we used in the previous chapter. In this chapter, we will not use any CSS, so do not mind that.

Create a file named `bootstrap-carousel.js` inside the `js` folder and import it in the HTML just below the `bootstrap.js` load (bottom of the page):

```
<script src="js/jquery-1.11.3.js"></script>
<script src="js/bootstrap.js"></script>
<script src="js/bootstrap-carousel.js"></script>
```

Let's create the plugin base. Inside the `bootstrap-carousel.js` file, add the following lines:

```
+function ($) {
  'use strict';

  // BOOTSTRAP CAROUSEL CLASS DEFINITION
  // =======================
  var BootstrapCarousel  = function (element, options) {
    this.$element = $(element);
    this.options = $.extend({}, BootstrapCarousel.DEFAULTS,
options);
  }

  BootstrapCarousel.VERSION = '1.0.0'
  BootstrapCarousel.DEFAULTS = {
  };

  BootstrapCarousel.prototype = {
  };

} (jQuery);
```

Here, we define a new function for jQuery. First, we define a class called `BootstrapCarousel` that will be our plugin. The function receives the element that will be applied the carousel and options that will be passed through data attributes or JavaScript initialization.

Why the plus symbol in the beginning of the function?

The plus (+) symbol forces to treat it as an expression so that any function after it should be called immediately. Instead of this symbol, we could use others unary operators to have the same effect (such as !, ~, or ( )). Without the initial symbol, the `function` can be seen as the declaration of a function rather than an expression, which can create a syntax error.

The variable options are then extended from the BootstrapCarousel.DEFAULT options. So, if an option is not provided, a default value will be used.

Let's define the VERSION of the plugin, the DEFAULT values, and the prototype that contains all the properties and methods for the class. Inside prototype, we will create the plugin methods and classes, and this is where the core logic will be stored.

Before creating the Bootstrap carousel logic, we must finish some tasks for plugin initialization. After prototype, let's create our plugin initialization:

```
+function ($) {
  'use strict';

  // BOOTSTRAP CAROUSEL CLASS DEFINITION
  // =======================
  var BootstrapCarousel  = function (element, options) {
    this.$element = $(element);
    this.options = $.extend({}, BootstrapCarousel.DEFAULTS,
options);
  }

  BootstrapCarousel.VERSION = '1.0.0'
  BootstrapCarousel.DEFAULTS  = {
  };

  BootstrapCarousel.prototype = {
  };

  // BOOTSTRAP CAROUSEL PLUGIN DEFINITION
  // ========================
  function Plugin(option) {

    var args = arguments;
    [].shift.apply(args);

    return this.each(function () {
      var $this = $(this),
          data  = $this.data('bootstrap-carousel'),
          options = $.extend({}, BootstrapCarousel.DEFAULTS,
$this.data(), typeof option == 'object' && option),
          value;
```

```
        if (!data) {
            $this.data('bootstrap-carousel', (data = new
BootstrapCarousel(this, options)));
        }

        if (typeof option == 'string') {
          if (data[option] instanceof Function) {
            value = data[option].apply(data, args);
          } else {
            value = data.options[option];
          }
        }
      }
    })
  }

} (jQuery);
```

The class `Plugin` will receive the `option` called and `arguments` for the element and call it. Do not worry about this part. This is quite a common plugin initialization that is replicated over almost all plugins.

To end the plugin initialization, add the following highlighted code after the `Plugin` class:

```
+function ($) {
  'use strict';

  // BOOTSTRAP CAROUSEL CLASS DEFINITION
  // =======================
  var BootstrapCarousel   = function (element, options) {
    this.$element = $(element);
    this.options = $.extend({}, BootstrapCarousel.DEFAULTS,
options);
  }

  BootstrapCarousel.VERSION = '1.0.0'
  BootstrapCarousel.DEFAULTS   = {
  };

  BootstrapCarousel.prototype = {
  };
```

```
// BOOTSTRAP CAROUSEL PLUGIN DEFINITION
// =======================
function Plugin(option) {
  .... // the plugin definition
}


var old = $.fn.bCarousel;
$.fn.bCarousel = Plugin;
$.fn.bCarousel.Constructor = BootstrapCarousel;



// BOOTSTRAP CAROUSEL NO CONFLICT
// ==================
$.fn.bCarousel.noConflict = function () {
  $.fn.bCarousel = old;
  return this;
}



// BOOTSTRAP CAROUSEL CLASS LOAD
// ==============
$(window).on('load', function () {
  $('.bootstrap-carousel').each(function () {
    var $carousel = $(this);
    Plugin.call($carousel, $carousel.data());
  })
})

}(jQuery);
```

First, we associate the plugin with jQuery by in the line `$.fn.bCarousel = Plugin;`. Then, set that the constructor for the class initialization will be called for `$.fn.bCarousel.Constructor = BootstrapCarousel;`. Here, we named our plugin bCarousel, so we will can the plugin via JavaScript:

```
$('some element selected').bCarousel();
```

Then, we add the plugin again for conflict cases where you have more than one plugin with the same name.

In the last part of code, we initialize the plugin via data class. So, for each element identified by the class `.bootstrap-carousel`, the plugin will be initialized passing the data attributes related to it automatically.

Defining the plugin methods

Now that we have our plugin well declared, we must fill the logic for it. We will create methods inside the `prototype` to create this behavior. We will only show this portion of the plugin code here.

The first method that we will create is `init()`. We will call it later to start the plugin. Before that, we have a few steps:

- Initial verifications
- Assigning the plugin elements and prerequisites
- Loading the original Bootstrap template
- Starting the Bootstrap plugin

The initialize method and plugin verifications

Actually, we have only one requirement from the Bootstrap original carousel plugin: the outmost `div` must have an `id`. Let's create the `init` function while making this assertion:

```
BootstrapCarousel.prototype = {
  init: function () {
    if(!this.$element.attr('id')){
      throw 'You must provide an id for the Bootstrap Carousel
element.';
    }

    this.$element.addClass('slide carousel');
  }
};
```

Therefore, we check if the element has the attribute `id` using `this.$element.attr('id')`. If not, we throw an error to the console and the developer will properly fix this issue. Note that we can access the plugin element using `this.$element` because we made this assignment at the start of the plugin.

In the last line of the function, we added some classes needed for the Bootstrap Carousel, in case we do not have it in the `$element` such as `.slide` and `.carousel`.

Adding the Bootstrap template

To load the Bootstrap Carousel template, let's create another function called `load` inside the `init` method to start it:

```
BootstrapCarousel.prototype = {
  init: function () {
    if(!this.$element.attr('id')){
      throw 'You must provide an id for the Bootstrap Carousel
element.';
    }

    this.$slides = this.$element.find('> img');
    this.$element.addClass('slide carousel');
    this.load();
  }

  load: function() {
  },
};
```

First, we must remove any Carousel elements that could be already present inside our `$element`. The elements that we must remove are the ones with the `.carousel-inner`, `.carousel-indicators`, and `.carousel-control` classes. Also, we have to load and hide the slide images in the variable `this.$slides`:

```
load: function() {
  // removing Carousel elements
  this.$element.find('.carousel-inner, .carousel-indicators,
.carousel-control').remove();

  // loading and hiding the slide images
  this.$slides = this.$element.find('> img');
  this.$slides.hide();
},
```

Next, we must make sure that there are not any other associations of Bootstrap Carousel in our plugin element. Append the following lines in the function:

```
this.$element.carousel('pause');
this.$element.removeData('bs.carousel');
```

First, we will pause the Carousel to stop any interaction and after use the function `removeData` in the `bs.carousel`, which is the name of the Carousel plugin.

To continue, we must load the Bootstrap Carousel template. Inside the class prototype, we have to create a variable to hold the original template. The variable will have the following format:

```
template: {
  slide: '…',
  carouselInner: '…',
  carouselItem: '…',
  carouselIndicator: '…',
  carouselIndicatorItem: '…',
  carouselControls: '…',
},
```

We are not going to place the full code of each template because it is quite extensive, and it would be better to you to check the full code attached with the book and see each template. Although there are no secrets in the templates, they are just a big string with some marked parts that we will replace. The marked parts are defined as a string around curly brackets, for example, {keyName}. When creating the template, we just need to replace these parts of the string by calling .replace(/{keyName}/, 'value').

Each key inside the template correspond to a certain part of the template. Let's explain each one:

- slide: This is the slide template of the new plugin and it is used to add slides via JavaScript

- carouselInner: This is the element inside the carousel that is parent for the items

- carouselItem: This is the item that contains the image and the caption of a slide

- carouselIndicator: This is the set of bullets at the bottom of the carousel

- carouselIndicatorItem: This represents each bullet of the indicator

- carouselControls: This is the controls to switch between left and right the carousel slides

At the end of the load method, add two more lines:

```
load: function() {
  this.$element.find('.carousel-inner, .carousel-indicators,
.carousel-control').remove();
  this.$slides = this.$element.find('> img');
  this.$slides.hide();
```

```
      this.$element.carousel('pause');
      this.$element.removeData('bs.carousel');

      this.$element.append(this.createCarousel());
      this.initPlugin();
   },
```

So, we will append in the `this.$element` the template generated in the function `createCarousel`. After that, we just need to initialize the Bootstrap original Carousel plugin.

Creating the original template

The original template will be created in the function `createCarousel`. It is composed of two steps. The steps are as follows:

- We create the slide deck for the `.carousel-inner` element
- Then, we create the indicator and the controls, if needed

Thus, the `createCarousel` method is composed of the call of these three functions that will append the string template to a variable:

```
createCarousel: function() {
  var template = '';

  // create slides
  template += this.createSlideDeck();

  // create indicators
  if(this.options.indicators) {
    template += this.createIndicators();
  }

  // create controls
  if(this.options.controls) {
    template += this.createControls();
  }

  return template
},
```

Note that for the indicator and the controls we made, check before creating the template. We performed a check in the `this.options` variable to see if the developer passed the argument to add these components or not.

So, we are defining the first two variables of our plugin. They can be passed through data attributes in the element, like `data-indicators` and `data-controls`. It defines whether the template will have these elements or not.

The slide deck

The slide deck will be created by the iterating of each `this.$slide` and loading the image source, the `data-title` and the `data-content` in this case. Also, for the first item, we must apply the class `.active`. The code is as follows:

```
createSlideDeck: function() {
  var slideTemplate = '',
      slide;

  for (var i = 0; i < this.$slides.length; i++) {
    slide = this.$slides.get(i);

    slideTemplate += this.createSlide(
      i == 0 ? 'active' : '',
      slide.src,
      slide.dataset.title,
      slide.dataset.content
    );
  };

  return this.template.carouselInner.replace(/{innerContent}/,
slideTemplate);
},
```

In each iteration, we are calling another function named `createSlide`, where we are passing, if the slide is active, the image source, the item title, and the item content. This function will then replace the template using these arguments:

```
createSlide: function(active, itemImg, itemTitle, itemContent) {
  return this.template.carouselItem
      .replace(/{activeClass}/, active)
      .replace(/{itemImg}/, itemImg)
      .replace(/{itemTitle}/, itemTitle ||
this.options.defaultTitle)
      .replace(/{itemContent}/, itemContent ||
this.options.defaultContent);
}
```

We performed a check for the title and the content. If there is no title or content provided, a default value will be assigned from this.options. Just like the indicators and controls, these options can be passed through data attributes such as data-default-title and data-default-content in the plugin HTML element.

> Do not forget that these options can be also provided in the plugin initialization through JavaScript by calling .bCarousel({ defaultTitle: 'default title' }).

The carousel indicators

The function createIndicators is used to create the indicators. In this function, we will perform the same method of the one to create the slide deck. We will create each bullet and then wrap it in the list of .carousel-indicators:

```
createIndicators: function() {
  var indicatorTemplate = '',
      slide,
      elementId = this.$element.attr('id');

  for (var i = 0; i < this.$slides.length; i++) {
    slide = this.$slides.get(i);

    indicatorTemplate += this.template.carouselIndicatorItem
      .replace(/{elementId}/, elementId)
      .replace(/{slideNumber}/, i)
      .replace(/{activeClass}/, i == 0 ? 'class="active"' : '');
  }

  return this.template.carouselIndicator.replace(/{indicators}/,
indicatorTemplate);
},
```

The only trick here is that each bullet must be enumerated and have a reference to the parent element id. Thus, we made the replacements for each this.$slides and returned the indicator template.

> **Why are replacing the key and surrounding with slashes?**
> Surrounding with slashes on JavaScript performs a regex search on the pattern provided. This can be useful for custom replaces and specific searches.

The carousel controls

The controls create the arrows to switch slides from left to right. They follow the same methodology as the other templates. Just get a template and replace the keys. This method must be implemented like this:

```
createControls: function() {
  var elementId = this.$element.attr('id');

  return this.template.carouselControls
    .replace(/{elementId}/g, elementId)
    .replace(/{previousIcon}/, this.options.previousIcon)
    .replace(/{previousText}/, this.options.previousText)
    .replace(/{nextIcon}/, this.options.nextIcon)
    .replace(/{nextText}/, this.options.nextText);
},
```

Note that in the first replacement for the {elementId}, our regex has an append g. The g on the regex is used to replace all occurrences of the following pattern. If we do not use g, JavaScript will only replace the first attempt. In this template we have two {elementId} keys, using which we replace both at once.

We also have some options passed through plugin initialization for the previous and next icon and the text corresponding to that.

Initializing the original plugin

After creating the original template, we must start the original Carousel plugin. We defined a function called initPlugin with the following implementation:

```
initPlugin: function() {
  this.$element.carousel({
    interval: this.options.interval,
    pause: this.options.pause,
    wrap: this.options.wrap,
    keyboyard: this.options.keyboard
  });
},
```

It just starts the plugin by calling `this.$element.carousel` while passing the carousel options on start. The options are loaded just like the others that we presented before. As shown, the options are loaded in the plugin class definition in the following line:

```
this.options = $.extend({}, BootstrapCarousel.DEFAULTS, options);
```

If any option is passed, it will override the default options present in `BootstrapCarousel.DEFAULTS`. We must create like this:

```
BootstrapCarousel.DEFAULTS = {
  indicators: true,
  controls: true,
  defaultTitle: '',
  defaultContent: '',
  nextIcon: 'glyphicon glyphicon-chevron-right',
  nextText: 'Next',
  previousIcon: 'glyphicon glyphicon-chevron-left',
  previousText: 'Previous',
  interval: 5000,
  pause: 'hover',
  wrap: true,
  keyboard: true,
};
```

Making the plugin alive

We are one step away from loading the plugin. To do so, create the following code in the HTML:

```
<div id="carousel-notification" class="bootstrap-carousel" data-
indicators="true" data-controls="true">
  <img src="imgs/doge.jpg" data-title="doge" data-content="Hey
there!">
  <img src="imgs/laika.jpg" data-title="laika" data-content="Hey
...!">
  <img src="imgs/cat.jpg" data-title="cat">
</div>
```

In our plugin JavaScript, we have to ignite the prototype by calling the `init` function like this:

```
var BootstrapCarousel   = function (element, options) {
  this.$element = $(element);
  this.options = $.extend({}, BootstrapCarousel.DEFAULTS, options);

  this.init();
}
```

Hooray! Open the HTML file in our browser and see the plugin in action, as shown in the next screenshot. In the DOM, you can how we perfectly mime the Bootstrap Carousel plugin, reducing the declaration in almost 35 lines of code:

Creating additional plugin methods

We are almost finishing our plugin. Now, it's time to add some methods to be called in the plugin, just like you can call `.carousel('pause')` on Bootstrap Carousel for instance.

When we were creating the plugin base, we created a class `Plugin`, which is the definition of the plugin. This part of the code is pretty common across the plugins and it is used on every native Bootstrap plugin:

```
function Plugin(option) {

  var args = arguments;
  [].shift.apply(args);

  return this.each(function () {
    var $this = $(this),
        data  = $this.data('bootstrap-carousel'),
        options = $.extend({}, BootstrapCarousel.DEFAULTS, $this.
data(), typeof option == 'object' && option),
        value;

    if (!data) {
      $this.data('bootstrap-carousel', (data = new
BootstrapCarousel(this, options)));
    }

    if (typeof option == 'string') {
      if (data[option] instanceof Function) {
        value = data[option].apply(data, args);
      } else {
        value = data.options[option];
      }
    }
  })
}
```

If you take a look at the highlighted lines of code, here we check the option variable that is passed. If it is a string, we `apply` the function, calling the option function on the plugin.

After that, we need to expose the function of the `BootstrapCarousel` class definition. So let's add two options, one to reload the plugin and another to add a slide to the carousel:

```
var BootstrapCarousel  = function (element, options) {
  this.$element = $(element);
  this.options = $.extend({}, BootstrapCarousel.DEFAULTS, options);

  // Expose public methods
  this.addSlide = BootstrapCarousel.prototype.addSlide;
  this.reload = BootstrapCarousel.prototype.load;

  this.init();
}
```

The highlighted lines represent the exposed methods. Now we need to implement them on the prototype.

Although one of the methods has already been implemented, the `BootstrapCarousel.prototype.load` when exposing it we renamed the expose from load to reload. Calling this method will erase all the Bootstrap Carousel original plugin, create the template again based on the images passed through our plugin, and generate the plugin again.

We need to implement the method `BootstrapCarousel.prototype.addSlide`. So, inside `Bootstrap.prototype`, create the following function:

```
addSlide: function(itemImg, itemTitle, itemContent) {
  var newSlide = this.template.slide
    .replace(/{itemImg}/, itemImg)
    .replace(/{itemTitle}/, itemTitle)
    .replace(/{itemContent}/, itemContent);
  this.$element.append(newSlide);
  this.load();
},
```

This function will receive `itemImg`, which is the source of an image; `itemTitle`, for the slide title caption; and `itemContent` for the paragraph on the caption as well.

To create a new slide, we first use the template for a new one that can be found in the template variable `this.template.slide`:

```
template: {
        slide: '<img class="hide" src="{itemImg}" data-
title="{itemTitle}" data-content="{itemContent}">',
… // others template variable
}
```

Like creating the slide deck, indicators, and controls, we set a multiple keys identified around curly brackets and do a replace of them in the function.

After the replacements, the new slide is appended to `this.$element`, which also contains the others slides. Finally, we need to call the load function, which will do all the hard work to assign variables, hide elements, and start the original plugin.

Then, when you want to add a slide to the plugin, you just need to call:

```
$('.bootstrap-carousel').bCarousel('addSlide', 'imgs/jon.png',
'New title image', 'This is awesome!');
```

With this plugin function, we are done! See, it is not too difficult to create a new plugin. We can now start incrementing it with more options for automation and customization.

Summary

In my opinion, this last chapter was awesome! We saw more about Bootstrap customization in terms of both components style and plugin interaction. Bootstrap is a great framework, but what makes it great is the extensibility potential that it has. It matches the perfect world where premade components and customization live in symbiosis.

To finish the book with a flourish, we developed a new Bootstrap plugin, the wrapper for Bootstrap Carousel. The plugin contemplates almost every pattern for the Bootstrap plugin, and it has been very helpful in creating a simple carousel with minimal verbosity.

The plugin is available on GitHub at `github.com/silviomoreto/bootstrap-carousel`. Take a look at it and create a pull-request! There are a bunch of improvements and new features that could be added to the plugin—perhaps a method to remove slides?

Also, the goal of creating a plugin is to make you able to create a new one in the future or understand a Bootstrap plugin if you need to adjust some part of it. I think you can now see the plugin's code with more familiarity and improve them.

I would like to congratulate you for reaching the end of the book. Understanding a complete framework such as Bootstrap is not a simple task and it is completed by just a small group of developers in the world. Be proud of your achievement.

The understanding of the plugin goes from the basic usage of the scaffolding from the creation of a plugin to the components, elements, and more. All of that was achieved using very useful examples that will be useful some day in your work.

The cherry on top of the pie is that you also learned about Bootstrap 4, which was released recently. This means you are one of the few people who are completely ready to use the new version of the Bootstrap framework.

I hope you liked the journey through the world of Bootstrap and were able to learn a lot from this book. Now it is your turn! You must go and nail every frontend Bootstrap task that you face. I believe that with all the knowledge acquired from the examples covered in this book, you are more than ready to be a true Bootstrap master.

Index

playing 125
thumbnails, using 131, 132
carousel
items, customizing 258
methods 261
options 261
options, URL 261
using 256-258
CDN setup
optional use 12
checkbox toggle buttons 272, 273
clearfix 41
community activity 13
contact form
about 81-83
JavaScript 83, 84
container tag 10-12
Content Delivery Network (CDN) 7

D

dashboard
about 198
charts, rounding 221-224
main content 219-221
quick statistical card, creating 224-226
spider chart, getting 227-229
devices
landing page, creating 51

E

Easy Pie Chart
URL 221
example
building 8, 9
container tag 9-12

F

flexbox
about 107-109
and Bootstrap 109
last navigation bar 199-202
URL 108, 110
fluid container 26

fluid content
advanced CSS 218, 219
collapse plugin 214-217
left menu 212, 213
main fluid content, filling 210
side stacked menu 211, 212
Font Awesome
URL 96
forms
contact form 81-83
forming 79
newsletter form 79, 80
sign-in form 85-87
framework
folder structure 4
sample example 4-6
setting up 3
tags 6-8

G

Glyphicon icons
about 95, 96
URL 93, 95
grid layout
about section 69, 70
changing 63
features section 71, 72
footer 76-78
forms, forming 79
grid system 65
header 65, 66
helpers 89
images 87, 88
introduction header 66-68
price table section 73-76
grid system 17, 18

H

helpers
about 89
context colors 89, 90
floating and centering blocks 89
responsive embeds 91
spacing 90

Highcharts plugin
URL 227

I

images 87, 88
input grouping
  making 105-107
italic elements
  usage 34

J

JavaScript plugins
  about 173
  data attributes 174
  JavaScript events 175
  library dependencies 174
jQuery
  URL 6

L

labels 169-171
landing page
  creating, for different devices 51
  desktop and large devices 59
  mobile and extra small devices 52-56
  tablets and small devices 57-59

M

main content
  feed, creating 134-139
  implementing 133, 134
  options, for pagination 140
menu affix
  creating 189
mobile design
  about 45, 46
  and Bootstrap 47
  and extra small devices 52
  landing page, creating for different
    design 51
  mess, cleaning 50, 51
  viewports, debugging 47-49

mobile viewport
  fixing 244-248
  missing left menu, adding 252, 253
  navigation menu, fixing 248-250
  notification list, styling 251
  round charts, aligning 254, 255
modals
  about 175, 176
  body 178
  custom modal, creating 179-181
  footer 178
  general and content 177
  header 177

N

navigation
  about 97
  adding 112-114
  bar, coloring 101
  collapse 98-100
  different attachments, using 100
  search input, adding 115
  time, for menu options 116
navigation bar
  customizing 118
  custom theme, setting up 118, 119
  finishing 120, 121
  list navigation bar pseudo-classes,
    fixing 119, 120
  some issues, fixing with 121-124
navigation bar, flexbox
  about 199-202
  finishing 204-208
  navigation search 203, 204
  profile, checking 209, 210
newsletter form 79, 80
npm file 3

O

overhead loading 230, 231

W

CPSIA information can be obtained at www.ICGtesting.com
Printed in the USA
LVOW09s1618190616

493089LV00007B/2/P